Things Which Become
SOUND
DOCTRINE

Things Which Become
SOUND
DOCTRINE

J. Dwight Pentecost

**ZONDERVAN
PUBLISHING HOUSE** OF THE ZONDERVAN CORPORATION
GRAND RAPIDS, MICHIGAN 49506

PREFACE

The Apostle Paul warned Timothy that "the time will come when they will not endure sound doctrine" and shall "turn away their ears from the truth, and shall be turned unto fables" (II TIMOTHY 4:3-4). He warned that men would "depart from the faith . . ." (I TIMOTHY 4:1). The antidote to this defection was to "Preach the word . . ." (II TIMOTHY 4:2). Titus, in a similar situation, was enjoined to "speak . . . the things which become sound doctrine" (TITUS 2:1). Instruction in the Word would preclude defection from the truth.

The day in which we live is marked by just such departures as Paul anticipated. It is an age in which men are "tossed to and fro, and carried about with every wind of doctrine . . ." (EPHESIANS 4:14). Certainly one major reason for the wavering faith of many is ignorance of the truth because of a neglect of the doctrines of the Word of God.

To strengthen the members of the congregation of Grace Bible Church of Dallas, Texas, of which the author is the pastor, the writer presented a series of doctrinal studies in the great words of our faith. Such was the response to these studies that, after rewriting and editing, they are presented in book form.

Grateful appreciation is expressed to the congregation of Grace Bible Church, who, like the Bereans, ". . . received the word with all readiness of mind . . ." (ACTS 17:11), which made the preparation and delivery of these studies such a joy. Deep appreciation is expressed to two of the Lord's servants, Mrs. Paul Allen and Mrs. Offie Bayless, who transcribed and typed the manuscript for publication.

May the Lord be pleased to use these studies to instruct the saints in the truths "which become sound doctrine."

DALLAS, TEXAS   J. DWIGHT PENTECOST

CONTENTS

Things Which Become
SOUND
DOCTRINE

... speak thou the things which become sound doctrine

—TITUS 2:1

1 ◆ Depravity

Galatians 3:17-24

THE AVERAGE BELIEVER feels that doctrine belongs in the seminary classroom or on the shelf of the minister's library, but is not to be brought over into the pew or into the daily living of the child of God. Yet, apart from a knowledge of the doctrines of the Word of God, we will continue in spiritual immaturity and will be tossed about by every wind of doctrine. There are certain great doctrinal concepts in the Word of God which every believer ought to know. He ought to be able to state the teaching of Scripture on such doctrines as grace, regeneration, substitution, redemption, justification, sanctification, and security, to mention but a few. It is our purpose in this series of doctrinal studies to present some of the truths of the Word of God in a simple and popular manner, precious truths that will be foundation stones upon which to build Christian lives. We trust that God will give you a hunger to enter into the truths of these great doctrines of the Word of God.

The first great doctrine of the Word to which we would direct your attention is the doctrine of *depravity*, or as it is popularly referred to, "total depravity." This doctrine has suffered from many misconceptions, for the average person would define total depravity by saying that it means that man is as bad as he can be. However, if we adopt that as an acceptable definition, immediately our theology is brought into question because we know men who are not as bad as they can be. We know many men who are good men, kind men, generous men, moral men, men who contribute much in the home and in the community. Rather, the doctrine of depravity says that man is as bad *off* as he can be. There is a vast difference between being as *bad* as he can be, and being as bad *off* as he can be.

The doctrine of depravity has to do, not with man's estimation of man, but rather with God's estimation of man. We are the heirs of generations of the teaching of evolution which sees man in an ever-ascending spiral, rising higher and higher from the depth from which he has sprung, until finally he will reach the stars. So widely accepted is that concept that we have come somehow to feel that there is so much good in the worst of us that man is not so bad off after all. When we measure men by man, we can always find someone who is lower than we are on the moral or ethical scale, and the comparison gives us a feeling of self-satisfaction. But the Scriptures do not measure men by man; they measure men by God who has created them. The creature is measured by the Creator and is found to be wanting. We would like to direct you to a number of Scriptures to see God's estimation of humanity, God's estimation of man outside of Jesus Christ, God's estimation of man as the result of the fall.

The doctrine of depravity has to do not so much with man's conduct as with man's state. It has to do not so much with man's behavior as with his condition before God. In Galatians 3:22 we read, ". . . the scripture hath concluded all under sin. . . ." In this passage we see that God has made a universal pronouncement, a pronouncement that characterizes every creature. The entire human race is classified as being *under sin*.

Now, in order to understand what it means to be under sin, we have to understand something of the aspects of sin presented in the Scripture. There are three aspects of sin presented in the Word of God. First of all, there is the aspect of personal sin which has to do with the acts which come from the individual, the manifestations of the exercise of the person's will. In Romans 3:23, the Apostle writes, ". . . all have sinned, and come short of the glory of God." This is a divine characterization of the unsaved man's life. All have sinned. And when God looked down upon the human race after the fall, He saw the race as a race of sinners, composed of those who are guilty of personal sin.

The Word of God uses a number of different words to describe the personal sins of the unregenerate man. The word *transgression* is used of a man's personal sin. It pictures man as stepping to one side, or overstepping the bounds of decency or propriety which God has marked off. Scripture refers to sin as *iniquity*, that which is altogether wrong. The word *error* is used, by which it is shown that the sinner disregards the right or goes astray from that which is the norm. The word *sin* is used of one's personal transgression and this refers to that which falls short of the mark or goes wide of the target. The word *wickedness* is used, and wickedness is the outworking and expression of an evil nature which is within man. The word *evil* is used and that refers to what is actually wrong or what opposes the goodness and the holiness of God. The word *ungodliness* is used for the man who lacks respect for God, who does not have a reverence or an awe for God. *Disobedience* characterizes the sinner and disobedience is an unwillingness to be led or guided in the ways of truth. The word *unbelief* characterizes the sinner and unbelief is the failure to trust in God. The word *lawlessness* is used for that which is in open contempt of divine law. Now, these ten words, all of which are used of the unbeliever, give us God's picture of the sinner and the aspects of personal sins of which the individual may be guilty.

The second aspect of sin, as it is used in the Word of God, refers not to the acts, but rather to the nature which produced the acts. This is referred to frequently as the sin-nature within the individual. When Adam was created and placed in the Garden of Eden, he was created a total person, with a full and complete personality. Adam was created with an untried innocence. Adam was created with a potentiality for evil but he was not created a sinner or a sinful being. A test of Adam's obedience was placed in the Garden, and Adam succumbed to the temptation of Satan and ate of the forbidden fruit. As a result, the nature of Adam was changed from untried innocence to a nature confirmed in sin. If I may use a common illustration, the nature of Adam in the Garden of Eden was like uncongealed gelatin. When Adam sinned, his nature was congealed and it became a sin-nature. When once that nature had taken on a permanent set, it was unalterable and unchangeable, apart from divine grace. The nature that was Adam's after the fall was a nature characterized by sin. When Adam's nature bore fruit, the fruit was characterized by God as being sinful fruit. Adam could do good things: he could love his wife, he could faithfully till the garden, he could be a good father to his children, he could be a good citizen in the society in which he moved. But when viewed from the divine standpoint, all that came from the root nature of

Adam was characterized by God as being sin. Since the root was corrupted, the fruit bore the corruption of that root.

At the time of creation God established the principle that like begets like: each was to produce after its kind. When Adam and Eve begot children, it was early manifested that those children were "after their kind," for Cain murdered his brother. The son received the nature which his father had to pass on to him and it was a sinful nature that manifested its true character in hatred that produced murder.

In the Epistle to the Romans, Paul speaks of the nature that is in an individual by his natural birth: "So then with the mind I myself serve the law of God; but with the flesh the law of sin" (7:25). Again, in Romans 8:2, he says, ". . . the law of the Spirit of life in Christ Jesus hath made me free from the law of sin and death." Now, the law of sin (7:25), and the law of sin and death (8:2), is the principle, or nature, which operates through the unregenerate individual. The fruits of the nature of man are characterized by God as sin and death. In Romans 3:10-18 the Apostle catalogues some of the fruits of that nature: "There is none righteous, no, not one: There is none that understandeth, there is none that seeketh after God. They are all gone out of the way, they are together become unprofitable; there is none that doeth good, no, not one. Their throat is an open sepulchre; with their tongues they have used deceit; the poison of asps is under their lips: whose mouth is full of cursing and bitterness: Their feet are swift to shed blood: Destruction and misery are in their ways: And the way of peace have they not known: There is no fear of God before their eyes." Again, in Galatians 5, the Apostle shows us the fruits of the nature with which one was born into this world, for in verses 19-21 he says, ". . . the works of the flesh are manifest, which are these; Adultery, fornication, uncleanness, lasciviousness, Idolatry, witchcraft, hatred, variance, emulations, wrath, strife, seditions, heresies, Envyings, murders, drunkeness, revellings, and such like: of the which I tell you before, as I have also told you in time past, that they which do such things shall not inherit the kingdom of God." In passages such as these Paul presents the truth that a man is not only guilty of personal sin, and therefore under judgment, but man has within him a fallen, sin-nature that prompts and produces personal sins; and for this nature man has come under judgment.

12

There is a third aspect of sin, referred to in Galatians 3:22; ". . . the scripture hath concluded all under sin. . . ." The phrase "under sin" refers to the state in which man has been placed by an act of God. Man is not only guilty of personal sin, and not only harbors a sin-nature within his breast, but man has been placed by God in the state of sin. Again we find this same truth presented in Romans 3:9 where the Apostle says, ". . . we have before proved both Jews and Gentiles, that they are all under sin." Man, in the Garden of Eden, was in a state of untried innocence. Man was in a state where fellowship with God was possible. Man was in a state where righteousness was obtainable. But when man disobeyed God and ate of the forbidden fruit, man was placed in the state of sin. That was his condition, his environment. You are an earthling, and live in the environment of this sphere; your whole being is conditioned to the atmosphere in which you live. The fish was designed for a different sphere and so differs greatly from a human being because it was designed to live in a different atmosphere. Man, by creation, was designed to live in the sphere of God. But when man disobeyed God, man's whole being was changed and he came to be in an entirely different atmosphere. His whole life now conforms to that atmosphere into which he was plunged by his sin. Man is not only a sinner by practice and a sinner by nature, but God has concluded, or God has set, all men in the state of sin. That is the divine classification. In Romans 11:32 the Apostle points out, as he did in Galatians 3:22, that men are in the state of sin by a divine decree. God has concluded them all in unbelief that He might have mercy upon all. In order that God's grace might be manifested toward men, God put all men in one classification or category. And God decreed men to be in the state of sin so that He might redeem sinners. If you refuse to accept God's divine judgment and decree that you are a sinner by practice, and possess a sin-nature, and have been placed in the state of sin, there is no redemption possible for you. From the Word of God, then, we learn this first great fact that contributes to our understanding of the doctrine of depravity; men are *under* sin.

The second great fact about men is that they are *spiritually dead.* In Ephesians 2:1 Paul affirms this fact: "And you hath he quickened, who were dead in trespasses and sins."

At the time of the creation of man, God affixed a penalty for man's disobedience. The penalty for disobedience was spiritual death. Physical death was the result of spiritual death. God said (Ezekiel 18:4), "... the soul that sinneth, it shall die." In Romans 6:23 Paul says, "... the wages of sin is death. ..." This is a truth which is well known and needs little repetition at this point. Let me remind you of Paul's teaching on this fact in Romans 5:12 where he says, "Wherefore, as by one man [that is, Adam] sin entered into the world, and death [physical death] by sin; and so death [physical death] passed upon all men, for that all have sinned." Now, when Paul says, "... all have sinned," he is not saying all have committed personal sins. That is a fact, but that is not what Paul is teaching here. Paul teaches that all sinned in Adam: we were in Adam at the time that Adam sinned. The theologian says we were seminally present in Adam. Because we were in Adam at the time Adam sinned, Adam's spiritual death passed to us. That is why we were born spiritually dead. Now Paul's argument, in the 12th verse, is the argument from the lesser to the greater: since men die physically, and they do, it is evident that men are spiritually dead, because physical death is the result of spiritual death. Paul affirms the fact that men do not die physically because they commit sins, but rather that they die physically because they died in Adam. And spiritual death is a part of this doctrine of depravity. We were not only under sin, but we are spiritually dead because we are in Adam.

The third great fact that the Scripture affirms is that the one who is under sin and spiritually dead is also *under condemnation*. May I quickly direct you to a number of passages that bring this truth to us. In John 3:18, John writes, "He that believeth on him is not condemned: but he that believeth not is condemned already, because he hath not believed in the name of the only begotten Son of God." And in verse 36: "He that believeth on the Son hath everlasting life: and he that believeth not the Son shall not see life; but the wrath of God abideth on him." Men are under judgment and under wrath because they are in Adam. The condemnation comes because we are in the state of sin. Or again, in Romans 1:18, the Apostle says, "... the wrath of God is revealed from heaven against all ungodliness and unrighteousness of men, who hold the truth in unrighteousness." There the Apostle affirms not only that men are under wrath because they are in Adam, but are under wrath because of the personal sins which they have committed. Or again, in I

Thessalonians 5:9, Paul, writing of the glorious hope that belongs to the children of God, says that God hath not appointed us to wrath. He affirms the fact that wrath is the part of the sinner who has no Saviour. In II Thessalonians 1:9, the wicked "shall be punished with everlasting destruction from the presence of the Lord, and from the glory of his power." In Galatians 3:13, "Christ hath redeemed us from the curse of the law, being made a curse for us: for it is written, Cursed is everyone that hangeth on a tree." The Apostle there affirms that Christ took our curse. If He took our curse it must mean that there is a curse upon those who know not Jesus Christ as a personal Saviour. These are but a few of the many Scriptures to which we could look which show us that the one who is in his natural state is under divine judgment, under a curse, under the wrath of a righteous God.

There is a fourth fact presented in the Scripture as a part of the doctrine of depravity. The natural man is under sin; he is in the state of death; he is under condemnation; but he is also *under the power of Satan,* under the control of the evil one. In I John 5:19, John says, ". . . the whole world lieth in the lap of the wicked one." In II Corinthians 4:4 Satan is called "the god of this world." In Ephesians 2:1-3 he is called "the prince of the power of the air, the spirit that now worketh in the children of disobedience." In Colossians 1:13 Paul writes, "Who hath delivered us from the power of darkness, and hath translated us into the kingdom of his dear Son." In these passages we see the truth presented that the one who is in Adam is also under the control of Satan: he is a part of Satan's family; he is in Satan's kingdom; he has his citizenship in Satan's cosmos; he is a citizen of a rebel state. Therefore, he has no relationship whatsoever to Jesus Christ.

Finally, we find that the doctrine of depravity presents also the truth that a man in his natural state is *lost*—L-O-S-T. There is perhaps no word as hopeless as the word *lost.* Yet that is the picture given to us of the natural man in his state of depravity. When our Lord would teach the nation Israel of God's attitude toward sinners, as recorded in Luke 15, He used three parables: the Parable of the Sheep, the Parable of the Coin, and the Parable of the Son. The thing that characterized each one of the three was that each was lost: the sheep was lost, the coin was lost, the son was lost.

The heart of the Father is revealed by Christ. The Father seeks the lost. Perhaps the lostness of the man outside of Christ is nowhere as thoroughly presented as in Ephesians 2:12 where the Apostle writes of the condition of the Gentiles who were outside of Christ: ". . . at that time ye were without Christ . . ."—that is, without a promised One who would be Redeemer and Deliverer—". . . being aliens from the commonwealth of Israel. . . ." It was to Israel that the promises were given of a King who would remove their sins before He reigned over them. Israel was the chosen nation, and the Gentiles were passed over. They were lost because they were without Christ. They were lost because they were aliens from the commonwealth of Israel. Paul continues: ". . . ye were . . . strangers from the covenants of promise. . . ." To no Gentile had God ever appeared and made a covenant promise, as He had with Abraham, to give his seed a land and a blessing. To no Gentile had God appeared, as He had to David, to promise One who would reign over them. To no Gentile had God appeared, as He had to Jeremiah, to promise that He would take away their sins and that their sins and iniquities He would remember no more. They were lost because they were strangers from the covenants of God. They were lost, Paul says, because they had "no hope." Hope was the settled assurance that God would send a Deliverer, a Redeemer, a Lamb who would take away the sin of the world. But to Gentiles no such promise was given. They were lost, finally, because they were "without God in the world." Gods they had, many, but they did not have one who truly was God. They bowed before idols of stone and of gold and of silver, but they did not bow before One who had life. And Paul writes the word LOST over the Gentile nations because they were under sin; they were spiritually dead; they were under condemnation; they were under Satan's power; they were *lost*.

Above the brink of Niagara Falls is a sign with a simple but arresting legend. It says, "Point of No Return." The Word of God says that men have slipped past the point of no return. They have gone over the cataract of sin, and have been swept into the state of sin. They are slaves of a sin-nature. They are producing the fruits of sin. They are spiritually dead; they are under judgment; they are under Satan's power. That is what it means to be depraved. Man is not as bad as he can be, but man is as bad off as he can be. He is lost. If you were left with only this picture, it could produce but dismay, for the doctrine of depravity does not give a ray of hope or

16

light, only despair and darkness. But after the Apostle has described the lostness of the Gentiles in Ephesians 2:12, he gives the glorious hope that is in the gospel when he says in verse 13, ". . . now in Christ Jesus ye who sometimes were far off are made nigh by the blood of Christ."

Jesus Christ is the only answer to the depravity of man. The answer is not in religion; the answer is not in a church; the answer is not in sacraments or ordinances; the answer to men's lostness is in a Person. As we were under sin by a natural birth, by a new birth we are placed in Christ Jesus. The man who was in Adam, and therefore under sin, has been placed in the Lord Jesus Christ. The man who was under condemnation has the promise: "There is therefore now no condemnation to them which are in Christ Jesus . . ." (Romans 8:1), for Christ has borne our judgments in His body on the tree. For those who were spiritually dead, Jesus Christ gives eternal life, and Jesus Christ's gift of eternal life is God's answer to our spiritual death. The one who has accepted Jesus Christ as his personal Saviour has been brought out from Satan's power, delivered from Satan's dominion, taken out of Satan's family, and has been brought into a new citizenship in the heavenlies, and has been brought into the family of God. The one who was lost has been found. Men's needs will be met, not by trying to soften the doctrine of depravity, not by denying the truth of the Word of God that men are under sin and spiritually dead, under condemnation, and under Satan's power. But men's needs will be met by presenting Jesus Christ so that those who were far off may be made nigh by the blood of Christ.

One of the most important questions which you can face is the question, "How far did Adam fall?" A number of different answers have been given to that question. The liberal says that Adam fell upward, so that Adam's lot was better after the fall than before the fall because something was added to the personality of Adam of which he had been deprived previously. Consequently, Adam was a fuller and more complete person after the fall than he was before the fall. There are those who say that when Adam fell, he fell over the cliff, but that when he was going over the cliff he grabbed something on the top of the cliff and held on. He fell downward, but he held on before he slipped over the brink, and if he exerts enough will and enough strength he can pull himself back up over the brink and stand on solid ground again. Those who have that concept are trying to lift themselves by their own bootstraps and work their way into heaven.

Then, there is the teaching that says that when Adam fell, he slipped over the brink, but he landed on a ledge part way down and that the ledge is the church and the church will lift him up and put him on solid ground again. But the Word of God says that when Adam fell, he fell all the way. He became depraved, totally depraved, unable to do anything to please God. He is under sin, dead, under judgment, under Satan's control; he is lost.

Beloved of God, in the Person of Jesus Christ as He is revealed through the Word, we have an answer to man's depravity. It is the Lord Jesus Christ who delivers from the state of sin, who removes condemnation, who gives us life for death, who brings us into His own family as the sons of God. I direct you to Him, the Saviour for depraved men.

2 ◊ Grace

John 1:6-17

GRACE IS GOD'S response to man's need. Born into this world with a sin-nature, under a curse, spiritually dead, in the Satanic world system and under control of its head, man's need was greater than man could meet. But to those who were in sin, God has manifest grace. In the second of our studies of the great doctrinal words of our faith we want to direct your attention to the doctrine of grace. The subject of grace is much larger than we could possibly consider in one brief study. For, from Genesis through the Book of the Revelation, you find manifestations of the grace of God. In Jeremiah 3:12 the prophet is told: "Go and proclaim these words toward the north, and say, Return, thou backsliding Israel, saith the Lord; and I will not cause mine anger to fall upon you: for I am merciful...."
I am merciful. The word translated "merciful" in Jeremiah 3:12 is the counterpart of the word that in the New Testament is translated "grace." God affirmed the fact that He is a God of grace.

There is a vast difference between being a God of grace and being gracious. Grace refers to the essential character of God and tells us what kind of God He is. Gracious*nesses* or gra*ces* come to an individual because of what the One gracing is within Himself. God is, first of all, a God of grace, and from a God of grace come multitudes of graces that meet our need. We might define grace as that intrinsic quality of God's being or essence by which He is spontaneously favorable in His disposition and actions. God is kindly disposed toward the sinner! This is the quality of the being of our God. All that comes to us from a God of grace, comes to us because He *is* a God of grace. God is kindly disposed within Him-

19

self, and this kind disposition spontaneously manifests itself apart from the desert of the one upon whom this grace is showered. God is a God whose disposition is such toward a sinner that, spontaneously, mercy flows out from Him to meet man's miseries. And because God *is* a God of grace, what He is causes Him to be favorable in His disposition and His works. God is a God from whom grace pours forth upon the sinner and the grac*es* or the graciousnes*ses* that come to us from God, because of what He is, are called *mercies* in Scripture. There is mercy for our misery.

When the Apostle writes, "Let us therefore come boldly unto the throne of grace, that we may obtain mercy, and find grace to help in time of need" (Hebrews 4:16), he is presenting three concepts within the word "grace." We, first of all, come to the throne of grace; the quality of God's being is imparted to the throne from which He rules the universe. Second, we may come with boldness unto the throne of grace to obtain mercy and find grac*es* to help in time of need. Third, because God is gracious, when we come to Him with our need God replies, not because of our merit, not because of the persistence with which we plead, not because of anything other than the need represented by the suppliant. Grace responds to our need.

From the opening chapters of the Old Testament we find revelations and manifestations of the grace of God. God created Adam and put him in a perfect environment. Adam was placed there with an untried innocence. Adam graciously was given the privilege of confirming himself through his obedience in the realm of grace. But Adam, by an act of disobedience, refused to be confirmed in a state of righteousness and became a lost sinner. At the fall of Adam we have the manifold mercies of God manifested as He demonstrated that He is a gracious God who pours out grace upon the sinner. In Adam's experience we see the manifold grace of God. In Genesis 2:17 God in grace postponed judgment upon Adam. In Genesis 3:15 God in grace promised One who would crush the tempter's head. In Genesis 3:16 God continued Adam as head of the race and as head of the family, even though he had sinned. This was an act of grace. In Genesis 3:19 God provided work for Adam, and this was an act of grace. God continued the usableness and usefulness of the earth, even though it had been cursed by Adam's sin, and this was a manifestation of grace. In Genesis 3:21 God provided a covering for

Adam's sin—an act of God's grace. In Genesis 3:24 God opened to Adam the prospect of access into His presence. There we read that God drove out man and He placed at the east of the Garden of Eden cherubim and a flaming sword which turned every way to keep the way to the tree of life.

The usual interpretation is to view these cherubim as policemen who were stationed at the entrance to the Garden of Eden to prevent Adam and Eve from coming back into the Garden again. I want to make a suggestion, although I will not dogmatize upon it. These cherubim with the flaming swords were not policemen to prevent the sinners from coming, but guardians to keep the way of access open. God, in the Garden, had set up a place of sacrifice where the lamb had been slain whose blood covered Adam's sin, and whose skin covered Adam's nakedness. That place of sacrifice was the divinely instituted place of meeting. Satan would have delighted to have closed that gate so that the way of access into the presence of God was barred to Adam. But God saw to it that the place of access was kept open so that Adam, through sacrifice, could come into the presence of God. God graciously kept the way open by which sinners could come into His presence. Thus Adam experienced the grace and mercy that came from God, the God of all grace.

We could point out that Abel received of the grace of God, for God had respect to Abel and to his offering, as it is recorded in Genesis 4:4. God was not obligated to receive the sacrifice, but graciously did so. Or again, in Genesis 5:24 we see the grace of God to Enoch, for God walked with Enoch and Enoch walked with God, and he was not, for God took him. This was an act of grace. We turn to Genesis 6:8 and we read that Noah found grace in the eyes of the Lord. This is the first specific mention of God's grace poured out upon man, although God had been gracious before the days of Noah.

Abraham knew much of the grace of God, for God's call issued to Abraham when he was in Ur of the Chaldees was a gracious call, because Abraham was born in the home of an idolator, and Terah, the father of Abraham, continued in his idolatry until his death (Joshua 24:2). It was not because Abraham was righteous that he was called, but because God was gracious. We find that Abraham was constituted righteous by the grace of God. Paul points out in

Galatians 3:6 that Abraham believed the promise and was constituted as righteous because he believed. Paul reminds us in Romans 4:5 that "to him that worketh not, but believeth on him that justifieth the ungodly, his faith is counted for righteousness." Abraham was called by grace; he was constituted as righteous by grace; and Abraham was given a covenant from God that promised him the land, and the seed, and the great blessing. This was a gracious covenant promise from God to Abraham. The covenant was not given to Abraham because Abraham was faithful—he wasn't. It was not given because Abraham's children would be faithful—they weren't. It was not given because Israel, the nation coming from Abraham, would be a faithful and obedient nation—they never were. The covenant was given because God was gracious. And all through the Old Testament, from the time of Abraham to the time of our Lord, God dealt in grace with the nation Israel, not because they deserved the grace of God, not because they were obedient, not because they were righteous, not because they were faithful, but because God was gracious. Because He had a covenant with them, as a faithful God, He would fulfill His promise even in spite of their unfaithfulness. God in grace responded to their disobedience by faithfulness. God responded to their sin by graciousness. God responded to their need in mercy. That is why the Prophet Jeremiah could write (3:12), "I am merciful, saith the Lord, and I will not keep anger for ever." *I am merciful.*

When we come into the New Testament we find the Apostle John emphasizing this theme of the grace of God. God's grace had been manifested from the time of the fall of man to the time of the fulfillment of the first promise to the sinner that God would send a Satan-Bruiser. But God's manifestation had been apart from a Person. God multiplied His mercies to men's miseries, and heaped up grace upon grace. Adam and Abel and Enoch and Abraham and Isaac and Jacob and Joseph and Job and David and Isaiah and Zechariah could testify to the grace of God. But the grace had never been manifest from God in the Person of the Son. After the coming of Christ, John can say, ". . . of his fulness have all we received, and grace for grace. For the law was given by Moses, but grace and truth came [put in their appearance] by Jesus Christ" (John 1:16-17) John does not mean to infer that there was no grace manifested under the old economy, for God has always been gracious and merciful; but now grace is personified and is paraded before men in the person of Jesus Christ. When the Lord manifested His grace to the miseries of men during His life, as recorded in the Gospels, we have multiplied witness to the grace of God in the Lord Jesus Christ. I think, for instance, of the publican who prayed (Luke 18:10) and would not lift up his eyes unto heaven but said, "God be merciful to me a sinner." Our Lord says he went down to his house justified. Why? There was grace and mercy for the sinner. I think of the sinful woman whose life is laid before us in Luke 7, and who came to anoint the feet of the Lord Jesus when the self-righteous Pharisees would give Him no water for ceremonial cleansing. She washed our Lord's feet with her tears. Christ said, "Thy faith hath saved thee . . ." (v. 50). There was grace for the sinner. I think of our Lord's teaching in the parables of the lost sheep, the lost coin, and the lost son in Luke 15. He shows us the grace of a Father who seeks that which was lost so that He might bring it to Himself. A gracious God responds to the lostness and misery of the sinner by seeking that which was lost. I think of the great supper in Luke 14, where those who were bidden would not come. The Lord said to go out into the highways and hedges and compel them to come in. There was grace for the sinner. I think of the laborers in the vineyard in Matthew 20. He sent some out early in the morning, and some at noon, and some in the evening, but He graciously bestowed His bounty upon all of them. I think of the thief on the cross to whom our Lord said, "To day shalt thou be with me in paradise" (Luke 23:43). Our Lord's life was characterized by the manifestation of mercy for the misery of men; by the display of the grace of God to those who stood under condemnation and judgment. In John 10 Christ pictured Himself as the good Shepherd who giveth His life for His sheep. Luke testified (19:10), ". . . the Son of man is come to seek and to save that which was lost." He came because He is gracious, and He came to bring grace to those who stood in need of manifestations of His mercy. I do not care what passage you turn to in the Gospels, you see grace heaped upon grace as the Son of God, the gracious One, met the needs of men with whom He came in contact. The grace of God is revealed in Jesus Christ. God is the Fountainhead, but Christ is the Channel through which it flows to men.

As in the Old Testament God had a basis for His manifestation of grace through His covenant which He established with Abraham, so in the New Testament God has a basis upon which He may manifest grace to man—the death of the Lord Jesus Christ. The Apostle Paul writes at considerable length and in many passages to present the different facets of the grace that has come to us from the God of all grace. We would like to point out briefly a number of the different facets of the truth presented by the Apostle as he magnifies his office as an apostle of grace. The first thing we would call to your attention is the fact that God has *manifested grace*. This is so self-evident that it may seem superfluous to you to mention it, but we want to remind you not only that God *is* a God of grace who spontaneously pours out favor in response to the miseries of men, but that God *has done so*. In Titus 2:11 the Apostle affirms the truth that "the grace of God that bringeth salvation hath appeared to all men." It is not a grace that is propounded as a theological proposition, but it is a truth that can be appropriated because it is a grace that has appeared. According to the first chapter of Ephesians, all that God has done in planning salvation, He has done to the praise of the glory of His grace. Salvation stands as the great demonstration that God—spontaneously, and apart from the merit and just deserts of the sinner—pours out mercy because He is a God of grace. Think of Paul's words in Romans 5:15: "For if through the offence of one many be dead, much more the grace of God, and the gift by grace, which is by one man, Jesus Christ, hath abounded unto many." Notice it—*the grace of God hath abounded unto many*. Or again, in verse 17, Paul writes, ". . . if by one man's offence death reigned by one; much more they which receive abundance of grace and of the gift of righteousness shall reign in life by one, Jesus Christ." They have received "abundance of grace." Or again, in II Corinthians 8:9, the Apostle reminds us that Christ has manifested the grace of God to men: ". . . ye know the grace of our Lord Jesus Christ, that, though he was rich, yet for your sakes he became poor, that ye through his poverty might be rich." Scripture gives abundant testimony that God *has* manifested grace.

In the second place, this grace which has been manifested is manifested in the *salvation* which God has provided. May we submit to you, beloved of God, that God's great manifestation and demonstration of grace is in the salvation which He offers to you. God's grace is not manifested principally through creation. God's grace is not manifested principally in other areas, although it is there. But God manifests His grace through the salvation which has been provided for you in Jesus Christ. Paul writes in Romans 3:24, "Being justified freely by his grace through the redemption which is in Christ Jesus"; he unites redemption, justification, and grace. Or again, in Romans 5:20, Paul says, ". . . where sin abounded, grace did superabound" (Author's Translation); the superabundance of God's grace is seen in the provision which God has made for those who were under the condemnation of the law. In Ephesians 2:5-8 Paul says, "Even when we were dead in sins, [God] hath quickened us together with Christ, (by grace ye are saved;) And hath raised us up together, and made us sit together in heavenly places in Christ Jesus: That in the ages to come he might shew the exceeding riches of his grace in his kindness toward us through Christ Jesus. For by grace are ye saved through faith . . ."; here the Apostle points out again that when God would manifest His grace, it is not by healing physical infirmities but by providing salvation from sin.

In the third place, when the Apostle speaks of grace he sometimes refers to the *state* into which we have been brought by the grace of God. I think of Romans 6:14 where Paul says, ". . . ye are not under the law, but under grace." Or again, of Romans 5:2: "By whom also we have access by faith into this grace wherein we stand. . . ." The Apostle points out that the believer who once was under law, under wrath, under condemnation, under the prince of this world, and under the god of this world, has been taken out from all that under which he had been placed and he is now put in a new state. He is under grace; he is in grace. As the unbeliever's sphere was the sphere of sin, so the believer's sphere of life is the sphere of grace. We live not under law, but in the sphere of grace. The air that we breathe, spiritually, is grace. The water that we drink, spiritually, is grace. The food that sustains us, spiritually, is grace. Our whole life is in the sphere of the grace of God.

Out of this grows, in the fourth place, the necessary corollary that grace is God's *operating principle* for His children. In the Word of God we have two principles contrasted. In the Old Testament you had the principle of law. Law was suited to infancy. As infants, the children of Israel had said, "We do not understand righteousness; we do not understand holiness; we do not understand the requirements which a holy God makes. Will you spell out for us what constitutes holiness?" So God gave them the law, which was suited to their spiritual infancy, in order that they might have a standard by which they could test the validity of any action to see whether it be right or wrong. In the New Testament, over against the principle of law, is the principle of grace, where God has taken us out from under the bondage of the law, which no man could keep, and put us under the principle of grace. Grace makes no less demands upon the child of God than law made; grace sets up as our standard the perfection of the Lord Jesus Christ and says, "This is what grace expects; this is what grace demands." And we are not less obligated to holiness and righteousness because we are under grace than if we had been under law. Child of God, the law under which Israel lived has been removed as a dominating principle, and grace is the operating principle. This is presented to us in Galatians 5:4 where the Apostle says, "Christ is become of no effect unto you, whosoever of you are justified by the law; ye are fallen from grace"—that is, if you return to law you have left the grace principle, the sphere into which you have been brought in grace. If grace no longer governs and controls your life, you are living under law. Grace, then, is the present operating principle.

As we continue, we find, in the fifth place, that grace *provides* for the daily needs of the child of God. We have already referred to this briefly when we directed you to Hebrews 4:16: "Let us therefore come boldly unto the throne of grace, that we may obtain mercy, and find grace to help. . . ." If you translated that second grace by the plural, you would get the thought in the Apostle's mind, for there are multiplied gra*ces* that come to us from the God of grace to minister to our needs every day. What needs do you, as a child of God, have? Are they physical? Are they material? Are they spiritual? God is the God of all grace, and He delights spontaneously to provide for your needs. It is because God is gracious and has graces for every need that the Apostle can be so confident and say, ". . . my God shall supply all your need according to his riches in glory by Christ Jesus" (Philippians 4:19). Do you think that that which God provides for you is that which you deserve? You don't deserve a thing. God provides for us in love because He is a Father and we are His children. But God provides because He is a gracious God and spontaneously responds to our need because such is His nature. He is a God of all grace for today's need.

Another fact that is presented to us in the Scripture needs emphasis; grace *cannot be compromised.* There can be no more union between law and grace than there is between day and night, between light and darkness, between black and white. Law and grace cannot be commingled, united together into a system that is part law and part grace. We affirm the truth of the gospel that it is not by works of righteousness which we have done, but according to His mercy He saved us, giving us the washing of regeneration, because He is a gracious God. In Romans 4:13-16 the Apostle says, ". . . the promise, that he should be heir of the world, was not to Abraham, or to his seed, through the law, but through the righteousness of faith. For if they which are of the law be heirs, faith is made void, and the promise made of none effect: Because the law worketh wrath: for where no law is, there is no transgression. Therefore it is of faith, that it might be by grace; to the end the promise might be sure to all the seed; not to that only which is of the law, but to that also which is of the faith of Abraham; who is the father of us all." It is of faith, that it might be of grace, to the end that it might be sure. If God covenanted to do ninety-nine percent of the work of salvation if you did one percent, you would have no certainty that you had accomplished your part of the bargain so that God could do His ninety-nine percent. You would live out your days in dread and fear because you would have no assurance that you had lived up to your part of the bargain. But, in order that salvation might be sure, God says it must be by grace. It is no wonder we delight to sing of the grace of God that brought salvation, for it is a gracious salvation that gives us certainty, security, and assurance.

When the Apostle speaks of the grace of God that has brought salvation, he includes within it all of the spiritual blessings that are ours in Christ. We are called by grace; we are justified by grace; we are sanctified by grace; we are sustained and kept by grace; we are equipped by grace; we are liberated from bondage, from sin, and from the law by grace; we are conformed to Christ by grace; we are reconciled by grace. God, in grace, has made a propitiation, a covering for our sins; God has provided redemption. List all that God has done and you find it is all the spontaneous outflow of grace as God bestows graces and mercies upon us in response to our need.

Men know something of pity. Pity is the response of an individual to the misery of another individual. God looked down upon us and

27

God pitied us. God pitied us because He is a gracious God; but whereas our hearts may be turned away, in spite of pity, from meeting the need of that individual, God spontaneously pours from Himself because He is an infinite God, an infinite provision for the needs of men. "For by grace are ye saved through faith; and that not of yourselves; it is the gift of God: Not of works, lest any man should boast" (Ephesians 2:9). No man will properly understand the infinite grace of God until he understands, first of all, his own need. That is why, before we speak on the grace of God, we speak of the depravity of man. In the Old Testament, Israel is commanded to look to the pit from which they were digged, the rock from which they were hewn. If you look to what you were outside of Jesus Christ, you see yourself as Scripture sees you: lost, without hope, without God, without promise, without assurance that God would meet your needs. Then, when you see God spontaneously pouring Himself out to meet that need, you have some concept of what it means to have received the grace of God. You had absolutely nothing within you to call forth God's spontaneous demonstration of mercy other than a need that you could not meet. And in response to that need, mercy has come from a gracious God.

There was one who had experienced this grace of God. He had been raised in a Christian home in England and in his earliest years had been taught the truths of a gracious God who bringeth salvation to all men. But he was orphaned at six years of age and he became, even as a small lad, a wanderer. He was raised by a non-Christian relative who scoffed at all he had been taught by godly parents. He became an apprentice seaman in order to get away from the conditions of the home of the relative and he joined the Royal Navy after he had served his apprenticeship. While he was enlisted in the Royal Navy he deserted and went to Africa, and he testified that he went for one purpose—to sin to his fill.

After he came into Africa, he joined himself to a Portuguese slave trader in whose home he was cruelly treated by the black woman who had become the chief of the harem. She took out her hatred for her Portuguese husband against this white lad and treated him like a dog. She exercised such authority over him that she threw his food on the floor and he was compelled to eat off the floor or be lashed. He fled from this cruelty and after escaping made his way to the coast where he attracted a ship by building a fire.

The ship's master was disappointed, for he thought that the fire meant that someone had either slaves or ivory to sell, but the young man was picked up, nevertheless. Because he was a skilled navigator he was made a mate on the trading vessel which was making its way up the coast of Africa to England. On one occasion, he opened the casks of rum and distributed to the crew so that the entire crew got drunk. The ship's master was so incensed that he had the mate thrown into chains. When he was brought up from below to be punished the captain treated him so brutally that he was knocked overboard and he was saved from death by drowning by the captain who threw a harpoon and speared him. He carried the scar of that deep wound, into which he could put his fist, until the time of his death.

As the ship made its way to Great Britain it was blown off course. When the ship began to flounder the young man was sent down into the hold to man the pumps along with the slaves who were being transported. He cried to God out of the hold of that ship. The truth he had been taught as a child came home to him and he came to know Christ as Saviour while he struggled over the bilge pump. It was this same John Newton who wrote the words:

> Amazing grace! how sweet the sound,
> That saved a wretch like me!
> I once was lost, but now am found,
> Was blind, but now I see.

Lost, but found! That can be your testimony if you do not know Jesus Christ as your Saviour. You may not have been as bad as John Newton, but you are as bad off as John Newton was in the sight of God. But God has grace for the sinner. God has mercy to offer to you in Jesus Christ, and we invite you to receive Him as your Saviour so that you might join in singing:

> Amazing grace! how sweet the sound,
> That saved a wretch like me!

3 • Regeneration

OF THE MANY experiences in a man's life to which he looks back with a great deal of fondness, certainly one of the outstanding is the moment his firstborn child is put into his arms. He holds that tiny form and looks down into that little, red, wrinkled, squalling face and says, "This is mine!" What dreams, hopes, desires, and ambitions fill a father's heart in that minute! Many times it has been a pastor's privilege to go into a hospital where a child has been born, and almost without exception, when the pastor has spoken with the mother and father, the father says, "Come on down the hall—I want to show you my baby," displaying that which is the father's joy. One never gets over the miracle of a human birth. We marvel at the miracle in the new life that has come into this world.

Heaven never ceases to wonder and to offer praise and thanksgiving to the God of creation, and the God of re-creation, for the miracle of the new birth. Our Lord spoke to Nicodemus and said, "Ye must be *born* again" (John 3:7). The Apostle, in Titus 3:5, said, "Not by works of righteousness which we have done, but according to his mercy he saved us, by the washing of regeneration, and renewing of the Holy Ghost." That which was referred to as being "born again" in John 3 is referred to as "regeneration" in Titus 3:5. The same truth is presented to us in another word, as found in Ephesians 2:1; the Apostle says, ". . . you hath he quickened, who were dead in trespasses and sins." The words "made alive," or "quickened," are the same concept as in "born again," or "regeneration." And frequently in the Word of God we have reference made to those who are the children of God. In I John 3 John said,

"Beloved, now are we the sons of God, and it doth not yet appear what we shall be" (v. 2); "Behold, what manner of love the Father hath bestowed upon us, that we should be called the sons [or children] of God . . ." (v. 1). And we are. And when reference is made to those who have been born into God's family as the children of God, Scripture is giving us the same basic concept as when our Lord said to Nicodemus, "Ye must be born again." In II Corinthians 5:17 we read, ". . . if any man be in Christ, he is a new creature. . . ." So whether we speak of born again, or a new birth, or regeneration, or quickened, or made alive, or sons of God, or a new creation, these words all bring before us the thought of the miracle of the new birth. It is that miracle of the new birth we would have you consider with us when we consider the doctrinal word, *regeneration*.

The English word *regeneration* is only a word of Latin origin which means "born again, born a second time, generated over again." And while we may be confused over the English word *regenerate*, there can be little confusion over "born again," or "born a second time," or "the new birth." One who is born into this world spiritually dead must be born a second time, of a new Father, into a new family, if he is to have eternal life and is to become the child of God. Human beings, apart from Adam, came into this world only one way, by a process of birth. This is the result of conception where the parents gave to the child the nature, the life, which they themselves possessed. If we are to be born into God's family, it must be through a miracle of a new birth, of a new Father who can give a new nature to us, so that we may be called the sons, or the children, of God. Now these are facts with which we trust you are very familiar, for there is no more important truth than that which Christ enunciated to Nicodemus: "You must be born again."

May we direct you to several passages in the Word of God which will emphasize different facets of this truth, so that you may see the complexity of this miracle. Human birth is a complex miracle, but the new birth is a far more complex miracle. That which we have come to take so for granted manifests to us the exceeding greatness of the power and the wisdom of God. In the first chapter of John's Gospel, verses 12 and 13, we read, ". . . as many as received him [that is, Christ], to them gave he power to become the sons of God, even to them that believe on his name: Which were born, not of blood, nor of the will of the flesh, nor of the will of man, but of God." Will you notice verse 13; leaving out the parenthetical and subordinate ideas, John states, "which were born . . . of God." And in this phrase "born of God" emphasis is placed upon the *Author* of the new birth. God is the Author of the plan of salvation. The Apostle Paul, in writing in I Corinthians 1:30, reminds us that Christ is the wisdom of God. Writing to the Romans in 3:26, Paul tells us that the salvation offered us in Jesus Christ is the manifestation of the wisdom of God, for God found a solution to the problem of how God could be just and at the same time justify the ungodly. The Author of our salvation is the all-wise God. Salvation was not an afterthought, as if after man sinned God found a way to patch up the rent in His plan; but salvation was ordained in Christ before the ages were ever formed. We were chosen in Christ, Paul tells us in Ephesians 1:3, before the foundation of the world, in order that God might manifest His grace, His love, His mercy, His wisdom, His justice, His righteousness, His holiness. God devised a plan whereby all that God is might be displayed in all its scintillating brilliance against the black background of sin. Salvation did not originate of blood; that is, it is not of human lineage. Salvation is not by the will of the flesh; that is, because a man sought God in his darkness. Nor is it of the will of man, as though man generated his own salvation. Man, dead in trespasses and sins, had no will toward God, no hunger nor appetite for God. He was self-satisfied, and self-complacent in his spiritual death. Salvation's plan did not originate with men, even in the minds of the wisest of men, but salvation originated with God. The Apostle John has eliminated every human instrument and agent, every human craving and desire. He says that as the child was born into this world, not because of his own will, but because of the will of another, so we are born into the family of God, not by the exercise of our own will, or of our own desires, or of our own working, but we were born of God. Reporting to us the message that was proclaimed by the Lord Jesus Christ, the Apostle records the fact that one is born of God. With this we may rightly begin our consideration of the doctrine of regeneration. *We are born of God.*

In the second place, as our Lord said to Nicodemus, "Except a man be born of water and of the Spirit, he cannot enter into the kingdom of God. That which is born of the flesh is flesh; and that which is born of the Spirit is spirit" (John 3:5-6). Here a very well-known truth concerning the new birth is presented. One must be born of the Spirit. God the Father is the Author, but the Holy Spirit is the *active agent* in the miracle of regeneration.

Water, through the Scripture, is used as an emblem of cleansing: we are cleansed with the water of the Word. Water is also used in the Bible as an emblem of the Word of God: the Word of God convicts of uncleanness, and that conviction brings us to One who can grant us cleansing, and through Him we enter into the experience of the new birth. While the Spirit may use means, the Holy Spirit is the active agent who accomplishes the new birth. As in human birth, there must be a human agent; so in the divine birth, there must be an agent, and the agent is the Holy Spirit of God. Since the Holy Spirit is one with the Father and the Son, and possesses the same nature as the Father and the Son, the one who is begotten of the Spirit is begotten, or is born, into the life of God and is endued with the nature of God. The agent, then, is not the flesh, for the Lord said in verse 6, "That which is born of the flesh is flesh. . . ." Two human parents can beget only one in their own likeness. They pass on, through this miracle of natural birth, the nature they received from their fathers, who in turn received it from their fathers, all the way back to Adam. That which is born of the flesh is always flesh. On the other hand, that which is born of the Spirit is spirit, and our Lord emphasizes the truth that, if we are to become children of God, we must have a new Father who can give us a new nature so that we can be acceptable in that new family. God is the Author; the Holy Spirit is the agent.

Now, that which the Holy Spirit begets is not a body, but rather is life. When we were born into this world by a natural birth, our parents were responsible for the life that we possess and also the body in which that life resides. When the Holy Spirit begets us into the family of God He does not beget a new body; that new body will come by resurrection. But the Holy Spirit does beget a new life, and the Spirit imparts the life of God as the life which is possessed by the child of God. It is the Holy Spirit's part, then, in this miracle of the new birth, to beget life.

As we turn to I Peter 1:23, we find the *means* by which the Holy Spirit produces the miracle of the new birth: "Being born again, not of corruptible seed, but of incorruptible, by the word of God,

33

which liveth and abideth for ever." There Peter refers to the use made of the Word of God by the Spirit in the new birth. We were born of God—God was the Author. We were born of the Spirit—the Spirit was the agent. But here we are born again by the Word of God, and the Word of God is the means by which the Spirit of God accomplishes the miracle of the new birth. In order to understand the part that the Word of God has, we must realize that Scripture claims to be a living thing. Hebrews 4 tells us that the Word of God is living, and powerful. Your English translation reads ". . . the word of God is quick, and powerful . . ." (v. 12), but "quick" means "living." The Word of God is living because it came from a living God and it has the power to impart life to those who are regenerated as the Spirit uses it as the agent. We are presenting to you "living truth" when we preach and teach the Word of God.

In addition to this fact, we must add Romans 10:17, where the Apostle Paul tells us that "faith cometh by hearing, and hearing by the word of God." We often hear men refer to "blind faith." We realize what men mean by that expression. They mean that we believe what we cannot see on the authority of the one who tells us a certain thing is true. But, really, there is no such thing as "blind faith." A man cannot believe that of which he is ignorant. He cannot accept that which he does not know. Before a man can have faith, he must have knowledge, and knowledge always precedes faith. If there is no knowledge, then faith has no object. The Word of God presents to us the truth of God. The Word of God gives us facts which faith may lay hold of. It is our ministry to teach the Word of God so that you may have some fact upon which you may lay hold and which will be the basis for your salvation, the basis for your daily life in the Lord Jesus Christ, as a child of God. Apart from knowledge, there can be no working faith.

The Apostle Peter tells us the part that the Word of God plays in our salvation, or in the new birth. The Word of God shows us why we need to be born again: we are sinners; as sinners we are under wrath, judgment, and condemnation. The sentence of death has been passed upon us and all who are sinners will be removed from the presence of God forever. They have no hope, no God, no Christ, no Saviour, no life. The Word of God shows us that Jesus Christ came to be the Saviour. The Word of God says that the Son of God was the sinless One who took our sins upon Himself. The Word of

God reveals that Jesus Christ has borne our griefs and carried our sorrows, that upon Him was placed all of our unrighteousness, that His righteousness might be given to us. The Word of God tells us that a man who does no more than believe that Jesus Christ is his personal Saviour passes from death into life. Those are all facts which are presented to you for your belief, that you might accept those facts and reckon upon them. Now, if you are ignorant of the Word of God, you are ignorant of your need of salvation; you are also ignorant of God's provision for salvation. Therefore, the Apostle Peter says, the Word of God has a part in salvation, for the Word of God reveals the fact, the need, and the solution to the problem, as it is found in the Lord Jesus Christ.

When we were born into this world the first time, we were born of corruptible seed. We were born from parents who had the corruption of Adam upon them. Going back to an earlier study in this series, we discovered that we were born into the world depraved. Our parents would have cleansed that line of corruption, had it been possible for them to have done so, and would have brought us into the world uncorrupted; but such was not in their power. If we are to be born into the family of God, we must be born of an uncorrupted, or incorruptible seed. And the Apostle affirms that very fact concerning the new birth: that we were born again the second time; not born of corruptible seed, as we were born the first time, but we were born of incorruptible seed, by the Word of God. That is why we make no apology for preaching and teaching the Word of God in its simplicity and in its power. When the Apostle came to the Corinthians he said, "I determined not to know any thing among you, save Jesus Christ, and him crucified" (I Corinthians 2:2). The Apostle said he came not with the persuasive words of man's wisdom or philosophy, for men by reasoning cannot find God. Men's theologies, men's philosophies, man's reasonings can never produce the new birth. That is why no new birth is possible where the Word of God is not preached.

I spoke to a couple just a few days ago who had asked me to come and call on them in order that they might ask me some questions. The questions that were upon their hearts were questions concerning salvation and forgiveness of sins. It was my privilege to sit down with them in that home, and to open up the Scriptures and go from passage to passage to show them what the incorruptible Word had to say about their need and God's solution to that need. After I had explained it to them, they turned to me and said, "We have been going to church for thirty years and we have never heard this." They had never been born again. Why not? Where the Word of God is not preached, there cannot be the miracle of the new birth, for the Word of God is the means which the Spirit of God, as the agent, uses to accomplish the new birth. It was my joy to see that couple come to Christ that night.

From this we pass to another word of Peter: where Peter says, "Blessed be the God and Father of our Lord Jesus Christ, which according to his abundant mercy hath begotten us again unto a lively hope by the resurrection of Jesus Christ from the dead" (I, 1:3). Again, may I leave out the subordinate phrases?—"He hath begotten us again . . . by the resurrection of Jesus Christ. . . ." Now, what part does resurrection have in the new birth? If you were to go into Romans 1:4, you would find that Jesus Christ was declared, or demonstrated, to be the Son of God, with power, by the resurrection from the dead. The resurrection of Christ, then, is the evidence of the exceeding greatness of God's *power* which worked on our behalf to bring us to salvation. In the first chapter of Ephesians the Apostle Paul looks to the resurrection of Jesus Christ as the greatest demonstration of the power of God that the world had ever seen, a demonstration that exceeded the creation of the universe. It was a power greater than the power that delivered more than two million souls from Egypt and sustained them through the wilderness. It was a power greater than the power that accomplished the miracle of the virgin birth. The greatest demonstration of the power of God that the world had ever seen was the resurrection of Jesus Christ from the dead, the ascension of Christ, and the official enthronement of Christ at God's right hand.

The Apostle says that we were begotten again by the same power that accomplished the resurrection of Jesus Christ. The new birth is a manifestation of the greatness of the power of God, and if there is a greater demonstration of God's power than the resurrection of Jesus Christ from the dead, it is your salvation. As great as was the miracle of resurrecting Christ after He had been made sin for us, an even greater manifestation of the power of God is the salvation of one sinner, for here is one who was lifeless, who was separated from God by a great gulf, who had no desire and no thought for God, who was satisfied and complacent in his sin and iniquity. But the Spirit of God laid hold upon that sinner and brought that sinner to faith in Jesus Christ; He accomplished the miracle of the new birth and brought that sinner into the family of God, as acceptable in God's sight as Jesus Christ is acceptable. That required the manifestation of the power of God.

When God redeemed the nation of Israel from Egyptian bondage, two great facts stood out about that redemption. First of all, it was a redemption by blood, for death laid hold upon the firstborn in every family where the blood was not applied to the door. But second, it was a redemption by power, for God overthrew the armies of the Egyptians; God opened up the way through the Red Sea so that the Israelites might cross on dry land to go into the wilderness. God preserved them for a generation until He brought them into the land, in fulfillment of His promise. That was redemption by blood and redemption by power. The Apostle Peter is emphasizing the fact that all of the infinite power of God is brought to bear in your salvation; and had Jesus Christ redeemed no other one besides you, your salvation would have been the greatest demonstration of God's power that the world could possibly see. But when you multiply millions of times over the number of those who have received Christ as Saviour, and have been born into the family of God, you have multiplied evidence of the exceeding greatness of His power to usward who believe. God is the Author; the Spirit is the agent; the Word of God is the means. The power of God was brought into operation to accomplish the new birth.

When we turn to Galatians 3:26, we discover yet another fact. We were begotten by faith: "For ye are all the children of God by faith in Christ Jesus." We become a child of God by only one way—by a new birth. And the Apostle points out, in the verse 26, that that which accomplishes the new birth is faith in Christ Jesus. Here we have the *instrument* by which the new birth is accomplished—faith in Christ Jesus. This same truth was stated by the Apostle John: "But as many as received him [received Christ], to them gave he power to become the sons of God, even to them that believe on his name" (1:12). Twice he states the instrument by which we became the sons of God: ". . . as many as *received* Him": ". . . them that *believe* on his name." This is the act of faith that simply stretches out the hand to receive that gift which God has to place in it. Belief,

37

or receiving, is the response to the facts of the gospel presented in the Word of God. Paul said he was not ashamed of the gospel of Christ, for it was the power of God unto salvation. When the power of God is revealed in the Word of God, and the fact is received and believed, then the miracle of the new birth takes place.

When Nicodemus came to Christ he was nonplussed by Christ's teaching that a man must be born again. Nicodemus began to reason concerning the new birth. You will recognize immediately that his natural reasoning was entirely erroneous, for he reasoned that the only way a man could be born again was somehow to re-enter his mother's womb and be born a second time.

Our Lord explained that the new birth takes place by faith. He used the illustration of the experience of the children of Israel in the wilderness. As a judgment from God because of their murmuring and complaining, because of their lack of faith and trust, the poisonous serpents moved among the multitudes and brought death. When Moses asked God for deliverance, God told him to lift up a serpent of brass upon a pole. And then He gave the instructions that anyone who looked on that serpent would be healed. The Israelites didn't have to work; they didn't have to pray; they didn't have to plead; they didn't have to make a promise; they didn't have to pay—they just had to look. And to look upon that serpent was to respond, in faith, to the message and the fact that Moses presented. Moses said, "This is the fact! Whoever looks will live." And they looked because they believed. And God, in faithfulness to His Word, caused life to come into those smitten bodies again. The Apostle John, in John 1:12, and Paul, in Galatians 3:26, say that this miracle of the new birth is not possible apart from faith—faith in a Person as He is revealed in the Word, so that the Author may send the agent, the Holy Spirit, to accomplish the new birth.

Finally, I Peter 1:17-19 gives the *basis* on which this new birth is accomplished. In verse 17, Peter says, ". . . if ye call on the Father . . ."—notice that word "Father," for it immediately establishes a Father-son relationship which is the result of the new birth. Now, on what basis may you call on God as Father? Verses 18-19 explain: "Forasmuch as ye know that ye were not redeemed with corruptible things, as silver and gold, from your vain conversation [or manner of life] received by tradition from your fathers; But with the precious blood of Christ, as of a lamb without blemish and without spot." You call on the Father because of the precious blood of Christ! The Apostle here is emphasizing the basis upon which God can cause this miracle of the new birth to be accomplished in your life. It is because Christ has given Himself as a sacrifice and an offering for your sins. It is because your debt has been paid. It is because God's wrath has been poured out upon Another and God's judgment against your sins has already been executed in the Person of Jesus Christ. A divine transaction took place at Calvary, a transaction in which all of your debts were gathered together, and Jesus Christ paid them to the full. Jesus Christ offered to the Father complete satisfaction for your sins and mine. The new birth, then, has as its basis the blood of Christ. Faith is the instrument by which the new birth is wrought. The new birth is the manifestation of the power of God. The means by which we are born again is the Word of God. The Holy Spirit is the agent which accomplishes the miracle. And the whole birth process is because God the Father desires to bring many sons into glory. God did not purpose to create a new race of beings to bring them into His presence. God could have created a whole new race, and brought them into heaven, but they would never have been sons, for one must be born with God as a Father before he can be a son.

In order that heaven might be populated for eternity with sons, God planned and provided for the miracle of the new birth. He sent the Spirit to accomplish the work. He gave His Son, that His Son might provide the basis for salvation by shedding His blood. He gives us the Word so that we might know the Son, that we might come, through faith, to a new birth.

Our Lord said to Nicodemus, "Ye must be born again." There is no greater message that the world needs. There is no solution but the solution which the Lord gave to Nicodemus: "Ye must be born of the Spirit." Have you been born again? Have you been regenerated? Have you become a child of God by faith in the Lord Jesus Christ because the Word has revealed your need, and has shown how Christ shed His blood, that your need might be met? You may become a son of God, in a moment of time, by faith in Him. Today can become your birthday, the day when you are born into God's family—if you will accept Jesus Christ as your Saviour.

4 ◆ Imputation

Hebrews 10:1-18

PAUL'S PRISON CELL in Rome became a pulpit from which the gospel went out to multitudes in the capital city of the Roman Empire. Among those to whom the gospel came in transforming power was a runaway slave, Onesimus, who had stolen from his master and made his way from the city of Colosse in Asia Minor over to Rome. While Paul could have used this newfound son in the faith to minister to his needs as a prisoner, he purposed to send Onesimus back to Philemon, his master. Paul wrote the letter to Philemon to exhort him to forgive and restore his runaway slave, and to count him as a brother in Christ. Paul recognized that before such a restoration could be made, the debt which Onesimus had incurred must be paid. Onesimus had nothing with which he could discharge that debt, and so in penning his epistle the Apostle says (vv. 17-18), "If thou count me therefore a partner, receive him as myself. If he hath wronged thee, or oweth thee ought, put that on mine account; I Paul have written it with mine own hand, I will repay it . . ." And in those words the Apostle was giving us a classic example of the great Christian doctrine of imputation.

The word "imputation" means to "reckon over to one," or "to set down to one's account." Paul is giving us an illustration of that which God has done for us in Christ Jesus. As the Apostle assumed the debt of Onesimus and invited Philemon—who had been wronged—to charge that debt to him, so the Lord Jesus Christ took the debt that we owed to the injured One—to God—and He charged Himself with our debt and set His righteousness down to our account.

40

While the word "imputation" does not occur with any frequency in Scripture, the ideas that constitute this doctrine abound throughout its pages. We want to bring together a number of concepts presented in the Word of God so that you might rejoice in the sufficiency of the provision which God has made for you in the grace kind of salvation which He offers you in Jesus Christ.

When God, as a divine Bookkeeper, begins to reckon our accounts, He spreads the ledger before Him, and as would be true in all accounting systems there is space for both credits and debits. God had to begin on the debit side of the ledger and He had to set down that which is actually ours. God, in all honesty, as a certified Accountant of the affairs of men, must deal with facts as they are. God begins the work of imputation by setting down to our account on the debit side the debt which we owe. In the fifth chapter of Paul's Letter to the Romans, we find the first great part in the doctrine of imputation. God sets down on the debit side of our ledger Adam's sin, for Adam's sin is imputed to all of Adam's race; Adam's sin is set down to the account of Adam's descendants. In this act God is imputing to us what is rightly ours because we are Adam's sons. In Romans 5:12 Paul writes, ". . . as by one man [that, of course, is Adam] sin entered into the world [the entrance of sin into the world is recorded in Genesis 3, where Adam rebelled against the command of God and ate of the forbidden fruit], and death by sin; and so death passed upon all men, for that all have sinned." The great act of imputation is implied in the words here translated "passed upon." Spiritual death is reckoned to our account. When God views us in our position in Adam, God sees us as spiritually dead. We were born spiritually dead because the parents who begat us physically were themselves spiritually dead and could pass to us only that which they had. The Apostle Paul emphasizes, then, that death entered the world because sin had entered the world, and that men die because Adam's sin is set down to each man's account on the debit side of the ledger.

In order to make this very clear, the Apostle shows us that men do not die because they are sinners, but, rather, they sin because they are sinners. He shows us in verse 13, "For until the law sin was in the world: but sin is not imputed [that is, sin was not counted transgression] when there is no law. Nevertheless death reigned from Adam to Moses, even over them that had not sinned after the similitude of Adam's transgression. . . ." Then, in the following verses, the Apostle shows that it was not the law that made men sinners; it was not breaking a law that made men sinners, because men were sinners, and men died before the law was ever given. Both physical death and personal sins had their root and origin in the sin of Adam. Because we were in Adam when Adam sinned, Adam's sin was set down to our account and we stand as guilty before God as though it had been our hand instead of Adam's that reached out to pluck the forbidden fruit from the forbidden tree in response to the enticements of Satan. We stand, therefore, before God, charged with Adam's sin. This is the act of imputation in which God sets down on the debit side of the ledger our indebtedness.

Before the books can be balanced, all of our indebtedness must be taken into account. It would be a relatively easy thing to balance our books at the end of the month and come out on the credit side, if we could choose to ignore all the larger bills that we have received during the month. But no accounting can be satisfactory which does not include all of the indebtedness that is against us. We have no right, when we have balanced the books at the end of the month, to announce joyfully that for once we are in the black, unless we have included every obligation that is against us. When God begins the divine work of salvation, He does not overlook some of the indebtedness. God does not treat sin as though it did not exist in the life of an individual. But God spreads His ledger and He makes an entry in that book that is all-inclusive. And the entry is "Adam's sin." Therefore, the first great fact in imputation is the fact that Adam's sin is imputed to the race. May we remind you again that God, in this act, is imputing to us what is already ours.

From this negative side we move on to the second great fact in imputation: the sin of the race was imputed by God the Father to God the Son. Here is a divine transferral in which that which did not belong to the Lord Jesus Christ was set down to the account of the Lord Jesus Christ. This, you will see, is just the opposite of God's first step in imputation. When God set Adam's sin to our account, He was setting down what was actually, or really, ours. Then God, in a second great act, set down to Jesus Christ what was not His. This was a judicial act in which my guilt, my sin, was placed upon Him.

Let us turn to several passages of Scripture which show us this act of God. May we turn back to the familiar chapter 53 of the prophecy of Isaiah, and there, hundreds of years before Jesus Christ was born, the prophet Isaiah portrays the One who would come as the Sin-Bearer. He tells us: "Surely he hath borne our griefs, and carried our sorrows . . ." (v. 4). The word "borne" means "to carry because something has been placed upon another." It is a word that would be used for a beast who bears a burden that has been placed upon its back. It is a word which would be used for a sorrow which one assumes for another and bears with him in sympathy. The Lord Jesus Christ is pictured as having borne *our* grief, *not His* grief, and having carried *our* sorrows, *not His* sorrows. Now how did our grief and our sorrows come to be borne by Christ? It was because God set down to His account what was not His, but what was ours. In verses 5-6, ". . . he was wounded for our transgressions, he was bruised for our iniquities: the chastisement of our peace was upon him; and with his stripes we are healed. All we like sheep have gone astray; we have turned every one to his own way [now, mark it well]; and the Lord hath laid on him the iniquity of us all." Here was a transferral; here was an imputation; here was a divine reckoning in which God the Father reckoned over to the account of God the Son that which was not rightly His.

In the Old Testament it was the custom for one to identify himself with the lamb that he offered as sacrifice by placing his hand on the head of that animal. You will recall that on the day of atonement the high priest took two goats and over the one goat he confessed the sins of the nation Israel, and he imposed his hands upon the head of that goat, and then that goat was led away in the wilderness. When the sins of the nation were confessed over that goat, and the high priest imposed his hands upon the head of that animal, the sins of the nation Israel were being borne by that animal. There was a reckoning over, there was an imputation of the sins of the nation to the scapegoat. When a father would call together his sons to give a paternal blessing, as Jacob did to his sons in Genesis 49, the father would put his hand upon the head of the son who was to receive blessing. By so doing, he was imputing, he was transferring blessing as he identified himself with his son by the act of placing hands upon the head.

Following that very familiar Old Testament picture, Jesus Christ is pictured in chapter 53 of Isaiah as the Lamb of God that would be sacrificed to bear away the sin of the world. He is pictured as the Scapegoat who bore away the sins. He is pictured as the One upon whom the Father placed His hands, confessing the sins of a guilty people, and the Father imputed, or reckoned to His account all the sins of the guilty ones so that Jesus Christ, as the Sin-Bearer, might bear our transgressions and iniquities away. He has borne our griefs and carried our sorrows because God the Father reckoned them over to God the Son. God hath laid on Him the iniquity of us all as God, by a divine act, transferred our sins to the Son so that the Son might bear them away.

Will you see the same truth taught again in II Corinthians 5:21, where the Apostle writes, ". . . he [that is, God the Father] hath made him [that is, God the Son] to be sin for us, who knew no sin; that we might be made the righteousness of God in him." For the moment we want to direct you to the first part of this verse: God the Father hath made Him to be sin for us. Will you observe, Paul did not say, "God the Father made Him to be a *sinner*"—for if Jesus Christ were a sinner, He could not be the sinner's substitute nor the sin-bearer. God the Father did not make Him a sinner, but God the Father made Him to be sin. God the Father reckoned over to His account all of the sins of Adam's race. Whereas Adam's race had imputed to them Adam's sin, that sin was transferred from the human race to the One who became sin. This was the divine act of imputation that reckoned over, or set to the account of Jesus Christ all of our iniquities.

Again, Peter writes of the same truth (I, 2:24-25), "Who his own self bare our sins in his own body on the tree, that we, being dead to sins, should live unto righteousness: by whose stripes ye were healed. For ye were a sheep going astray; but are now returned unto the Shepherd and Bishop of your souls." Here the picture is the same as we have seen in the previous references: to the Lord Jesus Christ was reckond over our guilt, our debt, our sin, our unrighteousness, and our uncleanness, that He might bear them in His own body upon the tree.

The Scripture has used different phrases—He has borne our griefs; God has laid on Him the iniquity of us all; God made Him to be sin; He bore our sins—and yet the thought in each one is identical in spite of the different English words. God has reckoned to Jesus Christ our sin. Take your stand at the foot of the cross and look up at the One who offered Himself as a sacrifice to God; and you cannot escape the fact that He is there as your Substitute. You cannot escape the fact that your sins were put upon Him and He is taking the place that you deserve, in order that He might give to you His gift of eternal life, forgiveness of sin, and righteousness from God.

That brings us to the third step in this great Scriptural teaching. Not only is Adam's sin imputed to the race, and the sin of Adam's race imputed to Christ, but, gloriously, the righteousness of Christ is imputed to believers. The righteousness of Christ is set down to the account of believers; it is freely reckoned over to the one who received Jesus Christ as personal Saviour. You see, in the first act of imputation God set down on the debit side of the ledger our indebtedness. In the second act of imputation, God erased the entry made in the debit side and set it down to Christ's account. In the third great act of imputation, God set down on the positive side of our ledger all the righteousness of Jesus Christ. Thus we might have a positive standing before God. Had imputation stopped with this second step, we would have been left with a record that was clean because the debit side had been removed; but there would still be no basis upon which God could receive us into His presence, for we did not possess a positive righteousness. But when the righteousness of Christ is imputed to us, a positive standing is given to us. This entry on the credit side of the ledger gives us the right to come into the presence of God.

In the first chapter of Romans the Apostle introduces the great theme of the Epistle. He is writing to the Romans concerning "the righteousness of God." Now he is not writing to tell us that God is righteous, but rather to tell us about the righteousness which God imputes to men through faith in the Lord Jesus Christ. In Romans 1:16-17 he says, "I am not ashamed of the gospel of Christ: for it is the power of God unto salvation to every one that believeth; to the Jew first, and also to the Greek. For therein [that is, in that gospel] is the righteousness of God revealed from faith to faith. . . ." The righteousness of God is revealed; not the fact that God is righteous —although the gospel affirms that truth—but the gospel reveals the righteousness of God that God imputed to the one who believes. We find this same truth in Romans 3:21-22: "But now the righteousness of God without [or apart from] the law is manifested, being witnessed by the law and the prophets; Even the righteousness of God which is by faith of Jesus Christ unto all and upon all them that believe. . . ." Again, in Romans 10:3 the Apostle says, concerning Israel, ". . . they being ignorant of God's righteousness, and going about to establish their own righteousness, have not submitted themselves unto the righteousness of God."

An incontrovertible fact presented to us in the Word of God is that God is a righteous God. And this righteous God in His work of salvation has a righteousness from Himself to impart—to impute, or to set down on the positive side of the ledger—to every guilty son of Adam's race. Here is a righteousness *from* God and it is the righteousness *of* God. We read in Romans 3:10 that apart from the righteousness of God, there is "none righteous, no, not one." Because Adam's sin is set down to all the human race, Adam's race is lost; Adam's race is unrighteous; Adam's race needs righteousness from God.

In this great act of imputation God is reckoning to the one who comes to Him through Jesus Christ that which is not his. Will you notice these steps again: first, Adam's sin is reckoned to the race (God is reckoning to us what is actually ours); second, God reckoned over the sin of Adam's race to Christ (God was reckoning to Him what was not His); and third, God reckoned the righteousness of God to the sinner (He is reckoning to that sinner what was not his). The act that set the righteousness of Christ to the account of the sinner is an act of free grace. In Philippians 3:8-9 the Apostle speaks of this great Divine reckoning: "I count all things but lost for the excellency of the knowledge of Christ Jesus my Lord: for whom I have suffered the loss of all things, and do count them but dung, that I may win Christ, And be found in him [note!], not having mine own righteousness, which is of the law, but that which is through the faith of Christ, the righteousness which is of God by faith." What does the Apostle say? He says that instead of self-righteousness and law-righteousness, God has set down to the sinner's account the righteousness of God which has become his righteousness by faith in the Lord Jesus Christ. Or again, in II Corinthians 5:21, the passage to which we referred earlier, the Apostle says, ". . . [God] hath made him to be sin for us, who knew no sin; that we might be made the righteousness of God in him"—that we might be *made* the righteousness of God! We were constituted sinners because of our relationship to Adam; we are constituted righteous because of our relationship to Jesus Christ. As Adam's sin was imputed to us on the debit side of the ledger (and that ledger was wiped clean because Jesus Christ bore our sins), so the righteousness of Christ is set to our account on the positive side of the ledger. God now has a basis by which He might accept us into His presence and receive us into His family as the beloved sons of God.

How could we be made the righteousness of God? Several passages will make this quite clear to us. In Hebrews 9:14 the writer says, "How much more shall the blood of Christ, who through the eternal Spirit offered himself without spot to God, purge your conscience from dead works to serve the living God?" I want to lift out the phrase, "offered himself without spot to God"—here the writer is viewing the divine transaction that took place on the cross. The Father had imputed to the Son all of the sin and the guilt of the world. The Son, bearing our sins, offered Himself as a sacrifice to God.

This is further explained in Hebrews 10:14: "For by one offering he [the Son] hath perfected for ever them that are sanctified." By this one offering Jesus Christ has provided for us the righteousness of God, available through faith in Himself. He is our Substitute. He has taken our sins upon Himself and He, in our place, has offered Himself as a sacrifice to God. Since the wages of sin is death, Jesus Christ went into death for us. He experienced physical death and spiritual death for us. He said, "My God, my God, why hast thou forsaken me?" The soul of the Son was separated from God— that was spiritual death. And when He said, "It is finished," and dismissed His spirit, He experienced physical death. Jesus Christ bore physical and spiritual death in our place, as our Substitute, in order that His righteousness might be reckoned over to our account.

Further, this righteousness can be ours because the believer has been placed *in* Christ Jesus. When we have been placed in Christ Jesus, we partake of all that Jesus Christ is. And since He is the righteous One, we partake of His righteousness, and the righteousness of God is our possession. In I Corinthians 1:30, the Apostle tells us that Jesus Christ "is made unto us wisdom, and righteousness, and sanctification, and redemption." Jesus Christ is made *right-*

eousness unto us. God "hath made him to be sin . . . ; that we might be made the righteousness of God in him" (II Corinthians 5:21). In Philippians 3:9 Paul says that we might have the righteousness of God by faith. In Colossians 2:9-10 Paul says, ". . . in him [that is, in the beloved Son] dwelleth all the fulness of the Godhead bodily. And ye are complete [fulness] in him. . . ." All that is in Jesus Christ is set down to our account on the positive side of the ledger because by faith we have been joined to Him and we have become His and He has become ours.

When a man takes to himself a bride he confers upon her all of the assets which he may have. The old-fashioned wedding ceremony used to have the man say, "With all my world goods I thee endow." All the position and the prominence that was his now was conferred upon his wife because she became one with him. The Lord Jesus Christ, in joining us to Himself, has conferred upon us not worldly goods but all His heavenly glory. Thus all that is in the Son is in the one who has been joined to the Son by faith in the Son Himself.

Imputation is God's method of bookkeeping. The sin of Adam is imputed to all of Adam's race and that indebtedness stands against a man and is the basis of condemnation. But Jesus Christ came and took Adam's sin upon Himself. Jesus Christ bore the guilt, the penalty, the curse of Adam's race, and offered Himself as a substitute to God. For the individual who receives Jesus Christ as personal Saviour, that record, which has been expunged from the curse of Adam's sin, has had set down on its positive side all of the righteousness of Jesus Christ. Your relationship to Adam has been canceled because that indebtedness has been imputed to Christ. You are now related to Christ, for Christ's righteousness was imputed to you. If you should be without Jesus Christ as your personal Saviour, you stand guilty before God because you are still in Adam's race. Even though Christ bore that sin, it means nothing to you until you are related to Him by faith. The righteousness of Christ cannot be imputed to you unless you personally receive Jesus Christ as your Saviour.

God has done a divine work. Even though it became necessary for God to charge Adam's sin to your account, Jesus Christ came and lifted that which was set to your account and bore it away. That is how John could say, ". . . he is the propitiation for our sins: and not for ours only, but also for the sins of the whole world" (I John 2:2).

He bore the sin of the world; the value of His death is for those who accept Him as personal Saviour. The righteousness of God is not imputed to the world; the righteousness of God is imputed only to those who have received Jesus Christ as a personal Saviour. We rejoice to proclaim to you the riches of the gospel, that the righteousness of God is imputed to men. We do not need to deny that men are sinners. We do not need to minimize the enormity of the debt of sin and guilt that rests upon an individual. Our salvation does not depend upon minimizing sin, but our salvation depends upon the divine work in which our sin, our guilt, was imputed to One to whom it did not belong so that all of His righteousness might be imputed to us. We can praise God for His divine reckoning. The Son said to the Father, "They have sinned. I do not plead for leniency. I do not ask You to ignore their sin. I offer a full and complete payment—charge it all to My account." And the Father, because of the payment by the Son, transferred our guilt and iniquity to the account of the Son, and transferred the righteousness of the Son to our account. The record is cleared because the debt was paid. We are accepted because His righteousness is imputed to us.

If you should be without Jesus Christ as your personal Saviour, you stand under Divine wrath, under the curse of God, for the sin of Adam has been set to your account. There you stand unless, by faith, you receive Jesus Christ as your Saviour so that He who has borne your guilt might set His righteousness to your account and make you acceptable before God.

5 • Substitution

Isaiah 53:1-12

FROM BEFORE THE creation of the world it was God's purpose to send His Son into the world so that His Son might display the infinite grace of God through His death. From the time of the fall of man all sinful creation had looked forward to the coming of the Redeemer. Since the death of Christ all look back to that event which is the pivotal point in divine history. The cross becomes the focal point of attention of both heaven and earth. As we see the Lord Jesus lifted up to die, we might well ask ourselves the question, "Why?"

We want to consider one of the important doctrinal words of our faith, the word *substitution.* Although this word nowhere occurs in our English text, yet a great body of revealed truth is encompassed in it. There is no more precious doctrine to which the child of God can give his attention than the doctrine of substitution. The necessity for substitution arises out of the righteous and holy demands of a righteous and holy God that sinners should be punished for their sins. At the time God created man and placed him in the Garden of Eden, a restriction was placed upon His creatures. God said, "Of every tree of the garden thou mayst freely eat: But of the tree of the knowledge of good and evil, thou shall not eat of it: for in the day that thou eatest thereof thou shalt surely die" (Genesis 2:16-17). A death penalty was affixed to this restriction laid down by God. In Ezekiel 18:4 the Prophet announced divine judgment: ". . . the soul that sinneth, it shall die." Familar are the words in Romans 6:23: ". . . the wages of sin is death; but the gift of God is eternal life through Jesus Christ our Lord."

It was a well-known principle, revealed throughout the Word of God, that a holy and a righteous God must execute the sentence which He had decreed upon sin. When Adam sinned and entailed the whole race in his sin, and when by imputation the sin of Adam was placed to the account of the race, it was necessary that God judge sin and that sinners be punished because of their transgressions. Yet our God is not only a holy, righteous, just, faithful, and true God; He is also a God of infinite patience, compassion, long-suffering, mercy, and grace. He is not a God who delights in the death of the wicked, but a God who delights in bestowing grace upon those who deserve only judgment and wrath. It is as though a conflict arose within the very nature of God. That conflict which poses the world's greatest riddle is set before us in Romans 3:23 when the Apostle Paul raises the question as to how God could be just, on one hand, and the Justifier of the sinner, on the other. How could God be faithful and true to Himself, His Word, and His character, and execute a just judgment upon sin, and at the same time redeem those who were sinners?

God found a way whereby He might be just, and at the same time the Justifier of the one who does no more than to believe. God's solution to this problem is in the doctrine of substitution. This doctrine presents to us the great truth of Scripture that God was faithful to Himself, and to His character, and to His Word to punish the sinner. But punishment on the sinner took place in the Person of a Substitute, so that God's judgment was meted out upon One who took our place. God, therefore, can receive the one who does no more than believe, because his sin was borne by a Substitute and his indebtedness was paid by Another. It is this vital doctrine which we would bring to your attention as we consider the Scriptural teaching on substitution.

First of all, let us touch on a number of passages of Scripture that present to us the concept of a substitute and present the doctrine of substitution. In the original text, the writers of the New Testament use a preposition which conveys to us the idea that one does something for another's good, or in another's behalf. When Jesus Christ is presented as the Substitute, in this sense, He is offering Himself for our benefit; He is performing an act for our good; He is performing a service on our behalf. The Apostle writes, in Luke 22:19-20, that Christ "took bread, and gave thanks, and brake it, and gave unto them, saying, This is my body which is given for you: this do in remembrance of me. Likewise also the cup after supper, saying, This cup is the new testament [or covenant] in my blood, which is shed for you." Now, when Christ said, "It is given *for* you," and "It is shed *for* you," He was saying, literally, "Here is a body which is given on your behalf, for your benefit, and here is blood which is shed for your good." At the time of the institution of the Lord's Supper, Christ was intimating the doctrine of substitution.

Again, in John 10:15, Christ said, "As the Father knoweth me, even so know I the Father: and I lay down my life for the sheep." We have the same expression occurring here as we find in Luke 22:19-20. And Christ said that when He, as the Shepherd, laid down His life, it was not for His benefit but for our benefit. It was not for the good which He could derive from that sacrifice, but for the good which could come to sinners through that sacrifice: ". . . I lay down my life for the sheep." Or, again, in Romans 5:8 the Apostle writes, "But God commendeth his love toward us, in that, while we were yet sinners, Christ died for us." The same word occurs again. Christ died on our behalf—for our benefit—so that good might come to us through His death. He endured the pain, the shame, the suffering, and the agony. The benefit was for us.

Again, in Galatians 3:13, Paul writes, "Christ hath redeemed us from the curse of the law, being made a curse for us: for it is written, Cursed is every one that hangeth on a tree." Jesus Christ was cursed—not because He merited a curse by God, for there was no sin in Him; the curse of God could not come upon Him for His own trangressions. But Jesus Christ was cursed on our behalf, for our benefit. Because He assumed a curse that was not His own, but a curse that was ours, the benefit and blessing of redemption and salvation come to us through Him.

In I Timothy 2:6 the Apostle writes, Christ "gave himself a ransom for all, to be testified in due time." The ransom has to do with the payment of a redemption price to set sinners free. Christ paid the price, not for the benefit that would come to Him through the purchase and possession of redeemed sinners; but Christ paid redemption's price for the benefit of those who were in bondage to sin. He became the Redeemer, not that He might be enriched by the possession of saved sinners; but He became a Redeemer, One who ransomed, so that the benefits might come to us through the payment of that ransom price.

Writing to Titus, the Apostle says that Christ "gave himself for us [for our benefit, for our good], that he might redeem us from all iniquity, and purify unto himself a peculiar people, zealous of good works" (2:14). The Apostle Peter emphasizes this great doctrine when he says, "For even hereunto were ye called: because Christ also suffered for us, leaving us an example, that ye should follow his steps" (I, 2:21). Or, in I Peter 3:18: "For Christ also hath once suffered for sins, the just for the unjust [or, on behalf of the unjust], that he might bring us to God, being put to death in the flesh, but quickened by the Spirit." And finally, Peter said (I, 4:1), "Forasmuch then as Christ hath suffered for us in the flesh, arm yourselves likewise with the same mind: for he that hath suffered in the flesh hath ceased from sin."

In all these passages to which we have called your attention, the common phrase "for us" is found. In this body of truth is presented to us the fact that Jesus Christ offered Himself without spot as a sacrifice to God—not out of some selfish motive, not because of what would come to Him through His offering, but for our good and for our benefit. Jesus Christ was not coveting the glory which would come to Him through His perfect obedience to the will of God. He was not thinking of the vast treasure of redeemed saints which would be given to Him by the Father as the Father's love-gift to the Son. Jesus Christ in His death had but one thought, and that was to provide for our good, for our benefit, for our blessing.

There is another line of teaching developed in the Word of God which contributes to our understanding. The Lord, speaking in Matthew 20:28, uses a different preposition—the preposition of direct substitution—where He says, "Even as the Son of man came not to be ministered unto, but to minister, and to give his life as a ransom for many." In our English text the word "for" might suggest only benefit, but in the original text our Lord has used the word for direct substitution. "The Son of man came not to be ministered unto, but to minister, and to give His life instead of many having to give their lives," is the thought. It is this emphasis, added to the previous line of teaching, that emphasizes the fact that Jesus Christ not only died on our behalf, that blessing and good might come to us from God through His death, but that Jesus

Christ actually died in our room and stead. Jesus Christ took upon Himself the guilt that was ours and endured in His own body the wrath that should have fallen upon us, and made an acceptable payment to God which God reckoned as our payment when by faith we accepted Jesus Christ as our Substitute. The Word of God very clearly teaches the doctrine of substitution.

There are other doctrines which must be considered along with the doctrine of substitution before we understand how God could count the death of His as a substitute for our death. We want to have you think with us first of all of Christ's incarnation among men, then of His identification with men, His separation from men, and then His substitution for men; for in this full-orbed relationship of Jesus Christ to men God has laid the foundation and the framework for the doctrine of substitution.

Consider, then, Christ's incarnation among men. From the earliest chapter of the Old Testament it was promised that a Deliverer and Redeemer would come. When God called Abraham, God revealed to Abraham that the Blessor would come from Abraham's seed. When the New Testament opened, Jesus Christ appeared as the Seed of Abraham. His physical lineage is traced in the first chapter of Matthew, and the third chapter of Luke, to show that Jesus Christ is the Son of David, the Son of Abraham, the Son of Adam. Jesus Christ, by His physical birth of the virgin Mary, is a Man among men. Through the virgin birth He possessed a full and complete humanity. This full and complete humanity was inseparably united with undiminished deity when the Theanthropic Person, the God-Man, came into this world among men. It is the fact of His identification with man that is emphasized by the writer to the Hebrews in the second chapter of that great Epistle. Beginning at verse 14 the Apostle said, ". . . as the children are partakers of flesh and blood, he also himself likewise took part of the same; that through death he might destroy him that had the power of death, that is, the devil." In this passage the writer is emphasizing the fact that Jesus Christ came to break the power of Satan over sinners, and to deliver men from the realm of Satan and the reign of death. In order to be the Redeemer and the Deliverer, it was necessary for the Deliverer to partake of flesh and blood; that is, the One who gave Himself for men must be a Man so that He could represent men. No animal could make a full satisfaction to God for the sins of men, for no animal was an equivalent substitute; no angel could offer satisfaction to God for the sins of men, for no angel was an equivalent substitute for a man. If Jesus Christ was to give His life as a ransom for the sins of men, it was necessary for Him to possess full, complete, undiminished humanity. Therefore the Apostle emphasizes the fact that since the children who need redemption have true humanity—that is, flesh and blood—it was necessary for Jesus Christ to have full, complete, true humanity. Therefore (v. 16-17) Jesus Christ did not take on Him "the nature of angels; but he took on him the seed of Abraham. Wherefore in all things it behooved him to be made like unto his brethren. . . ." Since Jesus Christ would give His life a ransom, not for angels, but for men, it was necessary for Him to take on not the nature of angels but the nature of men. That is why, earlier in this chapter, it could be said, "I will declare thy name unto my brethren . . ." (v. 12). Or again (v. 10), ". . . it became him, for whom are all things, and by whom are all things, in bringing many sons unto glory, to make the captain of their salvation perfect through sufferings." Since Jesus Christ would identify Himself with sinners, it was necessary for Him to be incarnate in the flesh.

We see this same truth presented in Hebrews 5:1: "For every high priest taken from among men is ordained for men in things pertaining to God, that he may offer both gifts and sacrifices for sins." The Apostle is emphasizing here a principle that before one can represent another, there must be an identity between the one representing and the one represented. If Jesus Christ is to represent men before God as a Priest, He must be a Man in order to represent men. When God gave a priest to the nation Israel, God reached down among one of the tribes of the children of Abraham and chose one family in that tribe, and made Aaron the first high priest. Aaron could represent his brethren because he was one of the brethren. And if Jesus Christ is to represent us before God, it will only be as He is incarnate among men and is possessed of a true humanity so that He may take man's place. When we look at the birth narratives given to us in the Gospels, we have not only the miracle of God come in the flesh; we have the groundwork laid for redemption, for Jesus Christ took on Him full and complete humanity that He might represent men in His death on the cross. The incarnation was a stepping-stone to substitution.

In the second place, we find that the high priest must be identified with men. This is emphasized again in Hebrews 5:2-3: the priest must "have compassion on the ignorant, and on them that are out of the way; for that he himself also is compassed with infirmity. And by reason hereof he ought, as for the people, so also for himself, to offer for sins." Earlier, in Hebrews 4:15, the Apostle writes, ". . . we have not an high priest which cannot be touched with the feeling of our infirmities; but was in all points tempted like as we are, yet without sin." Here the Apostle has affirmed the truth that before one can be a substitute for men, he must be so identified with men that he has experienced all that men have experienced, apart from sin, in order that he might be a faithful high priest.

In Matthew 3 we find the record of Christ's baptism. John the Baptizer had appeared in the wilderness and called out from the nation Israel a remnant who identified themselves as anticipating the Messiah, the Redeemer from sin. When Jesus came from Galilee to Jordan to John to be baptized of him, John forbade Him, saying, "I have need to be baptized of thee, and comest thou to me? And Jesus answering said unto him, Suffer it to be so now: for thus it becometh us to fulfil all righteousness. Then he suffered him" (vv. 14-15). The study of the baptism of Christ is a complex one, and it is not our purpose to go into the Scriptural teaching on Christ's baptism. We do want to emphasize this one important fact: John had identified a beliving group who confessed that they needed a Redeemer, who lifted voices in prayer that God would send His promised Messiah-Deliverer. Jesus came to be baptized by John so that He might identify Himself with those who were waiting upon God for a Redeemer. He took His place with men, and identified Himself with men, in order that He might represent men in His death on the cross. The baptism of Christ was an act in which Christ, the incarnate Son of God, identified Himself with men so that He might be numbered among them.

The record of the life of Christ reads like the record of a man: He became tired; He hungered; He thirsted; He knew sorrow; He knew rejection; He knew what it was to be spat upon and cursed; He suffered the indignities that the nation could heap upon Him. He identified Himself with all of the weaknesses, with all of the sorrows of men. The Apostle, writing to the Hebrews, says, ". . . in that he himself hath suffered being tempted, he is able to succour them that are tempted" (2:18). We have a faithful High Priest, because He was tested in all points, like as we are, yet without sin. Here we find the second step toward substitution: Jesus Christ was not only incarnate God come in the flesh, but He was identified with men.

That leads us to our third step. This we find in Hebrews, chapter 7: Jesus Christ was separated from men. In Hebrews 7:23-27 it is recorded, "And they truly were many priests, because they were not suffered to continue by reason of death; But this man, because he continueth ever, hath an unchangeable priesthood. Wherefore he is able also to save them to the uttermost that come unto God by him, seeing he ever liveth to make intercession for them." Note carefully these words: "For such an high priest became us [or, if I may translate it literally, 'for this kind of priest was the kind of priest that we needed'], who is holy, harmless, undefiled, separate from sinners, and made higher than the heavens; Who needeth not daily, as those high priests, to offer up sacrifice, first for his own sins, and then for the people's: for this he did once, when he offered up himself." The Apostle emphasizes that if Jesus Christ were only a man among men, He would not be an acceptable substitute for men, for the kind of substitute we need is One who is holy, and harmless, and undefiled, separate from sinners, and who has been placed at the right hand of the Father where He liveth to make intercession for us. If Jesus Christ is only a man, if Jesus Christ is begotten by natural generation, He is no acceptable substitute. He is under the curse and the wrath of God, as are you and I. One who is under the curse can not offer himself as an acceptable sacrifice for another. But the Apostle emphasizes that even though Jesus Christ came in the flesh, and even though Jesus Christ identified Himself with sinners in the flesh, He was separate from sinners so that there was no sin in Him. Those who were His enemies could not answer His challenge when Christ stood before them and said, "Which one of you convinceth me of sin?" (John 8:46). His friends who had walked with Him through the three and one-half years of His ministry had to testify that He did no sin, neither was guile found in His lips. The centurion who stood at the foot of the cross lifted his eyes to the One hanging on that central tree, and testified, "Truly, this was the Son of God" (Matthew 27:54). God rolled back the heavens and declared, "This is my beloved Son, in whom I am well pleased" (Matthew 3:17). And because Jesus Christ was separate from sinners, He was an acceptable substitute. Because He is God come in the flesh, because He identified Himself with men, and because He is separate from men, He could offer Himself as a substitute for men.

In Hebrews 2:9 the Apostle is presenting the truth: ". . . we see Jesus, who was made a little lower than the angels for the suffering of death, crowned with glory and honour; that he by the grace of God should taste death for every man." May we emphasize those words, "He tasted death for every man." Jesus Christ took upon Himself the sin of the world; He bore that sin to the cross. He bared His back not only to the blows of the Roman scourge; He received in Himself not only the mockery of the crowd; but He received in His body the wrath of God as it was poured out upon sin. And when Jesus Christ delivered Himself over to death, He did so conscious that He was bearing your sins and mine. He was conscious that the divine punishment meted out upon sin and upon sinners was falling upon Him because He, the spotless and sinless One, who was separate from sinners, had so identified Himself with sinners that it could be written by the Apostle Paul in II Corinthians 5:21, ". . . [God] hath made him to be sin for us, who knew no sin; that we might be made the righteousness of God in him."

This truth was so clearly anticipated by the Prophet Isaiah centuries before the Lord Jesus Christ gave Himself as a substitute in death. In that familiar chapter 53 the Prophet predicted the coming of the One of whom it could be said, "Surely he hath borne our griefs, and carried our sorrows: yet we did esteem him stricken, smitten of God, and afflicted. But he was wounded for our transgressions, he was bruised for our iniquities: the chastisement of our peace was upon him; and with his stripes we are healed. All we like sheep have gone astray; we have turned every one to his own way; and the Lord hath laid on him the iniquity of us all" (vv. 4-6). The Prophet Isaiah pictured One who would come as his substitute, and as ours, upon whom would fall the wrath of God so that God could be just in punishing sin, and the Justifier of all who will accept Jesus Christ's payment as their payment to God.

The doctrine of substitution had its first demonstration in the Garden of Eden when after Adam sinned, God slew a lamb, and the skin of a lamb covered Adam's nakedness, and the blood of a lamb covered Adam's sin. In God's provision of a lamb He portrayed the way by which He would make a final dealing with sin for all who would come under the blood of the Lamb of God. The lamb was Adam's substitute in the sentence of death. Abel's lamb anticipated the coming of God's Lamb. Every lamb offered upon Jewish altars in obedience to the Law of Moses anticipated the coming of God's Lamb. It was not until John the Baptist could point to the Lord Jesus Christ and say, "Behold the Lamb of God, which taketh away the sin of the world" (John 1:29), that God's acceptable sacrifice came among men. When Jesus Christ went to the cross, He went in order that He might fulfill God's eternal purpose of punishing sin, and yet might provide a basis by which sinners might be acceptable to God through His substitution.

Three crosses were prepared by the Romans for three malefactors. On two of the crosses thieves were to hang; the middle cross was prepared for a notorious criminal who had been guilty of treason against the Roman Empire. Yet Barabbas never found his way to that cross which had been prepared for him. Sentence had been passed upon him; he had been found guilty by the Roman court; of the just desert of his penalty there was no doubt; and yet another took his place. And on that middle cross that fateful day hung not Barabbas, the convicted criminal, but One in whose lips there had been found no guile. In the place of Barabbas there stood One of whom Pilate and Herod repeatedly had to say, "We find no fault in Him." And if Barabbas perchance had been attracted to that scene on Golgotha's brow, he could have looked up to that middle cross which had truly been prepared for him, and he could have said, "There hangs Another in the place that was rightly mine. I was adjudged guilty, and yet He is there instead of me." Barabbas went away a free man, not because he was innocent, but because Another took his place.

Sinner, you can stand at the foot of the cross as darkness descends over Calvary's brow, and you can look up to the One hanging on that middle cross and say, "That is the cross prepared for me. God rightly judged me as a sinner, and justly pronounced sentence upon me. But I go free because Another hangs there for me. He gave Himself for my benefit; He gave Himself in my place. He is my substitute."

It is not a question of your guilt or innocence, for you and all the world stand condemned before God. It is now only a question of whether you will accept God's substitute as your substitute, a question as to whether you will accept the death of the One who died on Calvary's cross as your payment to God for your sins. If you refuse the payment which God provided, then God will exact a payment from the one who should have paid it in the first place. Either Christ's death on your behalf, or your eternal death to satisfy the justice of God. Which will it be?

6 ◆ Repentance

I Thessalonians 1:1-10

THE GOSPEL IS characterized by its simplicity. When the Apostle Paul declared the terms of salvation to the Philippian jailer, he said "Believe on the Lord Jesus Christ, and thou shalt be saved . . ." (Acts 16:31). The Apostle Peter, speaking concerning salvation, declared, ". . . there is none other name under heaven given among men, whereby we must be saved" (Acts 4:12)—none other but the name of Jesus. Sinners, confronted with their need of salvation, frequently stumble over the very simplicity of the salvation which God offers. Since Satan cannot take away anything from the conditions of salvation or the plan of salvation—for God has already reduced it to an irreducible minimum—if Satan is to confound the minds of the sinners he must do so by addition, not subtraction. If conditions were placed by God to salvation, Satan might take away those conditions so that men would not be saved. But since there are no conditions, and salvation is a simple fact to be believed, Satan's method of deceiving men has been to add to the simplicity of the gospel. That is why some will teach that salvation is by faith and good works; or, salvation is by faith and baptism; or, salvation is by faith plus church membership; or, salvation is by faith plus repentance. These are all attempts to darken the mind of the man who needs to be saved concerning the central issue and the basic plan of redemption.

It is our purpose to discuss the Scriptural doctrine of repentance. It is important because so many minds have been confused concerning the simplicity of salvation by the perversion of the Scriptural teaching on this important doctrine. We trust that you will see from the Scripture not only the simplicity of the plan of salvation, but the part which repentance plays in the salvation of the soul.

We would like you to consider, first of all, the definition of the word "repentance." The doctrine has suffered tremendously from an erroneous concept held by most men, for when the word "repent" is used it brings to the mind of the average individual the thought of sorrow for sin. He pictures one down whose face course tears of remorse, and from whose lips come promises of change and a vow never to fall into the same sins again. And this sorrow for sins is usually called "repentance." But there could be nothing further from the concept of the Word of God than the idea that repentance means sorrow for sins. From the Word of God we discover that the word translated "repent" means "a change of mind." It means, literally, "a turning about"; not so much a physical turning about as a mental turning around, a change of course, a change of direction, a change of attitude. This is the concept in the word. Now, such a change of mind as the Scripture enjoins when it speaks of repentance may produce a sorrow for sin, but it will be the result after one has seen his sin in the light of the holiness of God and has changed his attitude toward it.

The Lord's parable will give us clearly the Scriptural concept of repentance. In Matthew 21:28-30 we read, "A certain man had two sons; and he came to the first, and said, Son, go work to day in my vineyard. He answered and said, I will not: but afterward he repented, and went. And he came to the second, and said likewise. And he answered and said, I go, sir: and went not." In this parable the first son, who had been commanded to go and work in the vineyard, said, "I will not," and afterward he repented. What did he do? He changed his mind. He had denied that which his father had requested and then he conformed to that which his father had commanded. That change of mind is repentance.

In II Timothy 2:24-25 we find the particular object that produces repentance. Paul writes, ". . . the servant of the Lord must not strive; but be gentle unto all men, apt to teach, patient, In meekness instructing those that oppose themselves; if God peradventure will give them repentance to the acknowledging of the truth." Now, in laying down the qualifications for the servant of the Lord, the Apostle emphasizes that the Lord's servant must have the ability to teach. That, of course, which he teaches—according to II Timothy

4:2—is the Word of God. As the servant of God teaches the Word of God, the truth of the Word of God will be brought home by the Spirit to the mind of the hearer, and the hearer will change his mind because of the truth that has been presented. This change of mind, in respect to a revealed truth from the Word of God, is called in II Timothy 2:25 "repentance."

In II Corinthians 7:10, the Apostle does show us that there is a relationship between sorrow and repentance, for he says, ". . . godly sorrow worketh repentance to salvation. . . ." You will observe from that verse that sorrow and repentance are not the same at all. Sorrow does its work, and when sorrow has done its work the product of sorrow is repentance and the product of the change of mind is salvation. The Apostle, then, has set up a progression: sorrow, repentance, and salvation. But the sorrow is not repentance, and the repentance is not salvation. From that verse we discover that repentance is not sorrow for sins; but rather, from the whole Word of God, we conclude that repentance is a change of mind, a change of attitude that does produce a change of direction in thought, in word, and in deed. If we were to be honest with ourselves, we would have to confess that most so-called repentance is not sorrow for sin at all, but sorrow for getting caught in our sin. Such a sorrow is not repentance, and we will miss the important teaching of the Word of God unless we are clear on the Scriptural concept that, in the Word of God, repentance is a change of mind.

There are a number of references we could cite to show that repentance is often used as a synonym for faith. In these passages you could eliminate the word "repentance" and substitute the word "faith" and it would not change the truth of the Word at all. The point to be observed is this: repentance is a change of mind toward the revealed truth of the Word of God. Previously a man disbelieved the revealed truth; and he has changed his mind and now accepts or believes the revealed truth, so that faith and repentance, on occasion, seem to be used interchangeably. Will you look at several references where this is true. In Luke 24:46-48 we read, "Thus it is written, and thus it behoved Christ to suffer, and to rise from the dead the third day: And that repentance and remission of sins should be preached in his name among all nations, beginning at Jerusalem. And ye are witnesses of these things." Now, what was to be preached? What were the preachers to call the people to do?

Why, in verse 47, they were called to believe that Jesus Christ had been raised from the dead; and instead of reading that "repentance and remission of sins should be preached in his name," if you understand the verse as "faith and remission of sins should be preached," you will do no violence to the text here. The revealed fact was to produce a change of mind, and those who had denied the resurrection are called upon now to believe the resurrection. But there must be a change of mind before they can believe. In Acts 11:18 we read, "When they heard these things, they held their peace, and glorified God, saying, Then hath God also to the Gentiles granted repentance unto life"—or, ". . . has granted a change of attitude toward the revealed truth, so that now they believe that truth, and the result of that change of mind that produces that belief is eternal life."

In Acts 20:21 we read that Paul was "Testifying both to the Jews, and also to the Greeks, repentance toward God, and faith toward our Lord Jesus Christ." A change of attitude toward the revealed truth of God that produced a faith toward the Lord Jesus Christ was the substance of Paul's teaching there before the Ephesian elders. Or again, in Acts 26:19-20, Paul testified before King Agrippa, "I was not disobedient unto the heavenly vision: But shewed first unto them of Damascus, and at Jerusalem, and throughout all the coasts of Judaea, and then to the Gentiles, that they should repent and turn to God, and do works meet for repentance." You will notice that the Apostle equates repenting and turning to God; there was a change of mind that produced a change of direction.

Again, in Romans 2:4, the Apostle says, ". . . despisest thou the riches of his goodness and forbearance and longsuffering; not knowing that the goodness of God leadeth thee to repentance?" Substitute the word "faith" for "repentance" and you will do no violence to the text. One more passage in this connection is II Peter 3:9: "The Lord is not slack concerning his promise, as some men count slackness; but is longsuffering to us-ward, not willing that any should perish, but that all should come to repentance." God desires that all should come to this change of mind that supplants unbelief by faith.

When, in these passages, we have equated faith and repentance, we would observe that a truth had been presented which had been disbelieved, and a change of mind brought a person from unbelief to belief, from rejection of the truth to faith in the truth. That is why faith and repentance may be used interchangeably.

We would next like to consider the concept of repentance in the Old Testament, for it is in this portion of the Word of God that a great deal of the confusion concerning the relationship of repentance to salvation arises. For our consideration, we are including in the Old Testament Scriptures all that took place before the death of Christ, and, for the purpose of our study, even those portions of the Word addressed to Israel immediately after the death of Christ; for we believe that the concept is the same in all these portions of Scripture.

In the first Gospel of the New Testament, you find that John the Baptist appeared suddenly on the scene in Israel with a startling announcement. He commanded and exhorted the people (Matthew 3:2): "Repent ye: for the kingdom of heaven is at hand." After he introduced our Lord, and our Lord identified Himself with the believing remnant in Israel by His baptism at the hand of John, Jesus began to preach and His message was identical to John's message as recorded in Matthew 4:17: "Jesus began to preach, and to say, Repent: for the kingdom of heaven is at hand." Both John, the forerunner of the Messiah, and the Messiah called upon the nation Israel to repent. John's message, as it is recorded in the third chapter of Matthew's Gospel, was a scathing denunciation of sin and sinners. But John did not call upon them to be sorry for their sins, nor to weep tears because their sins were being uncovered. John called upon them to change their mind concerning sin, concerning righteousness, and concerning their need of a Deliverer.

The nation Israel had been delivered over to rule by the Pharisees, and Pharisaism told the people of Israel that they were righteous because they were the children of Abraham, and that God would deliver any child of Abraham from going down into the pit. Pharisaism was a system of works; if a man observed the three hundred and sixty-five negative commandments, and the two hundred and fifty positive commandments, as the Law was summarized by the Pharisees, the Pharisees assured him he was safe. Our Lord denied that there was righteousness in Pharisaism, and demanded that the people turn to God to receive righteousness from Him. In that portion we call the Sermon on the Mount, our Lord said, ". . . except your righteousness shall exceed the righteousness of the scribes and Pharisees, ye shall in no case enter into the kingdom of heaven" (Matthew 5:20). These people were trusting Pharisaism for righteousness; they were trusting the Law of Moses for righteousness. Christ said that if you are ever to be made righteous you must change your minds as to the source and the means of righteousness. Righteousness is not in Pharisaism, nor in the Law, but it is in the Messiah who offers His righteousness to you. Men needed to change their minds about their own need. They were complacent in their self-righteousness, for the Pharisees counted themselves and their disciples as righteous before God. Our Lord and John preached to the nation that there was need for a change of mind: a change of mind concerning sin, a change of mind concerning righteousness, a change of mind concerning their need, that they might come to God to receive God's forgiveness.

In Matthew 22 we find that our Lord pronounced a judgment upon the nation because the nation would not repent. Whole multitudes professed to repent as they received John's baptism, but there was no true change of mind. That was evident, because there was no change of life as the result of the change of mind. And the nation to whom Christ had given a call to repentance repudiated Him as God's heaven-sent Messiah, and continued to trust in their own righteousness. In Matthew 21:43-44 Christ said, "The kingdom of God shall be taken from you, and given to a nation bringing forth the fruits thereof. And whosoever shall fall on this stone shall be broken: but on whomsoever it shall fall, it will grind him to powder." This was our Lord's announcement of judgment upon those who refused to repent and had rejected Him.

And then, in Matthew 23:37-38 our Lord says, "O Jerusalem, Jerusalem, thou that killest the prophets, and stonest them which are sent unto thee, how often would I have gathered thy children together, even as a hen gathereth her chickens under her wings, and ye would not! Behold, your house is left unto you desolate." Christ announced judgment upon the city of Jerusalem and upon the institutions within the city. The Temple, the priesthood, the Sanhedrin that had condemned Him—all would come under divine judgment. That judgment fell in the year A.D. 70 when Titus and his Roman legions, as the instruments of divine judgment, marched in and conquered the city, and destroyed and dispersed the people.

As we come over to the Books of Acts we find frequent exhortations to repentance. Peter, preaching in Acts 2, proclaimed the resurrection of Christ, proved the resurrection from the Old Testament Scriptures, and concluded in verse 36 "that God hath made that same Jesus, whom ye have crucified, both Lord and Christ [Messiah]." So convincing and convicting was Peter's message that we read in verse 37: ". . . when they heard this, they were pricked in their heart, and said unto Peter and to the rest of the apostles, Men and brethren, what shall we do?" And then Peter gave his answer, which has caused so much confusion in the world today: "Repent, and be baptized every one of you in the name of Jesus Christ for the remission of sins, and ye shall receive the gift of the Holy Ghost" (v. 38). Based upon a misunderstanding of this passage, some teach that apart from repentance (that is, a sorrow for sins) and water baptism there is no forgiveness for sins. There are large denominations which teach that apart from repentance and baptism there is no salvation. Now, what is the truth that Peter is proclaiming when he says, "Repent, and be baptized every one of you in the name of Jesus Christ for [or, with a view to] the remission of sins"?

Remember, our Lord and John had demanded of the nation Israel repentance (a change of mind) toward sin, toward righteousness, and toward judgment. The nation Israel refused to repent and the nation Israel came under judgment from the hand of God. No less than the Son of God had predicted the judgment that would come upon Jerusalem and upon the citizens of the land of Israel. When Peter convinced the men that Jesus was Lord and Messiah, and they cried "What must we do?" Peter said, "Repent; that is, change your mind. Change your mind about Christ. Change your mind about the Person who invited you to repent, but whose invitation you rejected." Peter was not asking for sorrow for sin—it was too late for that. He was asking them to change their minds concerning the truth that he had just presented—that Jesus is Lord and Messiah.

As long as they were in the nation Israel, and were citizens in good standing, they were under the temporal judgment which the Son of God had predicted would come upon that city and her people. And Peter said, "The only way you can escape the judgment that the Son of God has predicted will fall upon this city is for you to terminate your citizenship in this nation." Their citizenship could be terminated by baptism in the name of Jesus Christ. Those believers who had changed their minds about the Person of Christ severed their relationship to the nation Israel by baptism; by that act, they were cut off from the people who were to be judged and they identified themselves with the One about whom they had changed their minds. This they did with a view to receiving His forgiveness of sin. This exhortation to repent and be baptized, although applicable throughout the age, had its peculiar and particular application to that nation, to that generation under divine judgment, so that judgment might be escaped by individuals who heeded the truth Peter presented and who turned unbelief in the Person of Christ to belief, witnessing that faith, that change of mind, by separating themselves from the nation that was under judgment.

We find much the same truth presented in Acts 3:19 where Peter once again declared the glorious truth of the resurrection of Jesus Christ: "Repent ye therefore, and be converted, that your sins may be blotted out, when [so that] the times of refreshing shall [may] come from the presence of the Lord"—repent and be converted; or change your mind and be turned around. You can visualize this very graphically if you put the Law on one side and Jesus Christ on the other. The nation Israel had turned their backs on the invitation of Jesus Christ and were marching toward the Law, trusting it for their salvation. When they stood convinced that Jesus was actually the Messiah, Peter said, "You must change your mind and be converted, turned around, and you must begin your walk toward the Lord Jesus Christ, away from that to which you were going a moment ago." Repent and be converted, or change your mind and be turned around, so that the seasons of refreshing may come from the Lord. Thus we find that the call to repentance was addressed to a guilty nation in covenant relatonship with God, but whose responsibilities under those covenants were not being fulfilled. John and Christ invited the nation to Himself so that they might receive righteousness from Him; but before they turned to Him they must change their mind about their own righteousness, about Pharisaic righteousness, about Law righteousness, about their need for salvation. After the rejection of Israel brought Christ to the cross, He still offered that nation repentance, a change of mind, as the basis of forgiveness for sins.

We find that repentance has its place in the life and experience of the child of God. I would like to take you into the familiar passage in I John 1:9, a passage to which we come again and again: "If we confess our sins, he is faithful and just to forgive us our sins, and to cleanse us from all unrighteousness." You may be quick to say, "But I don't see the word 'repentance' there." No, I grant you, it is not there, and yet its concept is, for the Greek word translated "confess" is the word which means "to say the same thing." And confession is saying the same thing about our sins that God says about them. Repentance is involved in this act, for one must turn from his own evalution of his conduct to accept God's evaluation of his conduct before he ever acknowledges that what he did was sin. And so, in the believer's experience, there is a place for repentance, a place for a change of mind, if we are to know the blessed experience of restoration to fellowship through confession of sin.

It is in II Corinthians 7:8-10 that the Apostle speaks at some length concerning repentance in relationship to the believer. You will recall the background. Paul had written earlier, in a very strong tone, concerning sin in the life of the assembly. He had been somewhat distressed as to what reception his strong language would receive. He wrote, ". . . though I made you sorry with a letter, I do not repent [change my mind], though I did repent [change my mind]: for I perceive that the same epistle hath made you sorry, though it were but for a season. Now I rejoice, not that ye were made sorry, but that ye sorrowed to repentance: for ye were made sorry after a godly manner, that ye might receive damage by us in nothing. For Godly sorrow worketh repentance to salvation not to be repented of: but the sorrow of the world worketh death." Here the Apostle is showing the relationship between sorrow and repentance, and he says that a godly sorrow—that is, a sorrow that is produced because the child of God views his sin as God views it—will lead to a change of mind toward that sin. What he loved, he now hates; what he grasped after, he now repudiates; what governed and controlled his life and became the goal of his life, he now abandons, so that as he confesses his sin he receives forgiveness from God. Paul shows that sorrow is a prerequisite to repentance, but that sorrow is not identical with repentance.

We want to consider now something of the relationship of repentance to salvation. It is here that the great doctrinal battle has been fought as to whether salvation is by faith alone, or whether salvation is by faith plus something. There are approximately 150 passages in the New Testament that tell us that salvation is by faith alone; that salvation is the gift of God to one who will accept Jesus Christ as his personal Saviour. The Apostle writes and shows us that "to him that worketh not, but believeth on him that justifieth the ungodly, his faith is counted for righteousness" (Romans 4:5). And over against that great body of revealed truth there are still some who insist that apart from sorrow for sins, there is no such thing as salvation for the individual. I am certain you have been in meetings when an evangelist, or pastor, invited people to come to the altar and weep their way through to God—suggesting that apart from tears, crying, supplication, tarrying, and begging, there could be no forgiveness for sin. Sincere they are, but misguided, because they do not understand the teaching of the Word of God on this subject. Repentance is not a prerequisite to salvation; for if repentance is required, salvation is based, at least in part, upon works. The sorrow is the product of the human emotions, and it is the responsibility of the individual so to stir up his emotions that he can lay the foundations, or the groundwork, on which salvation will be built.

This interpretation is erroneous because it suggests to us the false concept that God is basically unwilling to receive sinners, that God is adamant and unapproachable in His attitude toward sinners, and that unless one softens the heart of God by tears, God is unwilling to accept him and grant forgiveness for sin. The common saying that "Tears are a woman's mighty weapon" becomes a basis for teaching that tears are the sinner's mightiest weapon to soften the heart of God and get an unwilling God to grant a gift that He is not disposed to impart. This denies, of course, the doctrine that God is propitious, that God is gracious, that God has extended His mercy to sinners, and that whosoever will may come.

Or again, this interpretation is wrong because it suggests that the death of Christ is not a sufficient basis for the forgiveness of sins; that God bases salvation upon the death of Christ plus sorrow, the death of Christ plus tears, the death of Christ plus praying and pleading; and that apart from those additions there can be no real forgiveness for sins. The word of God makes it very clear that salvation is based upon the value of the death of Christ apart from anything that the individual might add to it.

What part, then, does the change of mind, or repentance, have in salvation? We would suggest to you from the Word of God that repentance is included in believing. It is not a separate act which conditions salvation, but rather it is included in the act of believing; for when one believes a fact, he turns from doubt or unbelief to faith in that revealed truth. I think this is seen very clearly in I Thessalonians 1:9, where Paul said, ". . . ye turned to God from idols. . . ." This is one act. There are not two acts herein—only one; but the one involved the other. Notice, very carefully, what Paul said and what he did not say. Paul did not say, "Ye turned from idols to God." Had Paul stated it that way, two acts would have been involved: ye turned *from* idols—Act Number One; ye turned *to* God—Act Number Two. If there were two acts here, you could terminate the process in the middle. For instance, a man could turn from idols, and stop there, without turning to God. And so, the Apostle is not saying that you took two steps. Rather, Paul said, you turned to God from idols—that is one act. The turning to God involved the abandonment of the idols, but it all is one act.

This word "turning" gives us this basic concept that we have been considering. There was a change in attitude, a change of mind. The people had known no God but idols. Then Paul came to them to present the truth of God. They turned from their idols to believe the truth that had been revealed, and the Apostle says that the act gave them salvation. As a consequence they waited "for his Son from heaven, whom he raised from the dead, even Jesus, which delivered us from the wrath to come" (I Thessalonians 1:10). In the passage, the change of mind was not the precursory step to salvation. It is not the first of several steps to salvation. It is not a prerequisite for salvation. Rather, salvation depends upon believing, and believeing involves repudiating the false teaching that one espoused, and holding to the revealed truth of the Word of God. From Scripture, then, we see that salvation is predicated upon faith. Faith involves the repudiation, or turning from all falsehood, from every false basis of salvation, from every false hope, and turning to accept from God the gift of salvation through His Son. But salvation is not dependent upon the work of repentance; rather, it depends upon the faith that involves repentance.

71

Salvation will be preceded by repentance. The one who turns to God accepts God's judgment upon sin, accepts the fact of his need of a Saviour, accepts the fact of his guilt, accepts the fact of his lostness apart from Christ, accepts the fact of his helplessness. He turns from all self-righteousness in which he trusted, turns from his own works, turns from his church as a means of dispensing salvation, and turns to the Lord Jesus Christ, accepts the fact of God's judgment upon sin and sinners, and by faith receives Jesus Christ as the One who is judged for him. On many occasions it has been my privilege to open up the Word of God to men and women to show them that they were lost and under God's condemnation because of their unrighteousness, and to show them that God offers salvation to men through Christ. I have had the joy of hearing them say, "I accept Jesus Christ as my personal Saviour." Almost invariably emotion so chokes the individual and he is so overcome that he cannot restrain tears with the wonder of the fact that he has been born into the family of God. I sat, just a few days ago, with a man who in desperation asked if I could give him some hope. In simple faith he turned to the Lord Jesus and he had no sooner accepted Christ as his Saviour than tears began to flow down his face. They had no part in obtaining the salvation, but they flowed from the salvation which God had provided.

Salvation is by faith. Salvation does not depend upon sorrow for sin; salvation depends upon faith in the Lord Jesus Christ who offered Himself as a sacrifice for the sins of the world. If you are without Christ as your Saviour, salvation does not depend upon some emotional experience in which you work up sorrow for your sins; it depends on a changed mind. You have rejected Him; you have repudiated Him; you have trusted in your own righteousness, your own works, your own way, your own wisdom. Apart from a change of mind toward the truth of the Word of God, there is no salvation for you. Salvation must be preceded by that change of mind, but salvation is not based upon that change of mind. Salvation depends on your faith in the Lord Jesus Christ. Will you accept Him as your Saviour, and step out of death into His marvelous life?

7 ◆ Redemption

I Peter 1:3-20

THE RETURN OF a victorious general to the city of Rome transformed the staid and austere atmosphere of the city into a festive occasion. When a Roman general had been victorious over an enemy, he returned to Rome at the head of a great triumphal procession. He led back in triumph not only the forces that had served under him, but he also brought back the spoils of the conquered land as well as a large number of captives. All these formed the great triumphal procession. When the news of the victory reached the city of Rome, preparations would be made for the conqueror's return, for it was a time in which the glory won by the conqueror was heaped upon his head. He rode into the city to be received by the nobles and the dignitaries in a manner becoming his victory.

This was a time to which the wealthy looked forward, for they could buy from the spoils of conquest the treasures that would adorn their homes. It was a time anticipated by the slave owner who desired to enlarge the number of his slaves, for after the captives had been led in the triumphal procession, they would be taken to the slave market and there, one by one, would be put upon a slave block where they might be examined and tested by prospective buyers, and then purchased to be brought into a life of bondage and servitude.

It was this concept of slaves in a slave market which was uppermost in the minds of the Apostles as they spoke of the great work of the Lord Jesus Christ as a Redeemer and the work of redemption which He had provided for sinners. The Word of God looks upon men who are in sin as bond-slaves. It looks upon them as being under a master who has conquered and subdued them, and who can deliver them over to even greater bondage. The Scripture views the sinner as without any will of his own, indentured to serve sin and to be a bond-slave of Satan, to do whatsoever Satan demands. Jesus Christ has come into that slave market in order that He might purchase those who are in sin's chains, so that He might set them free. "Redeemed, How I Love to Proclaim It!" is a song we delight to sing. We lift our voices to extol not only the Redeemer but the redemption which He has provided. But we will never be able to praise our Redeemer for His redemption until we understand our condition in sin, our need of redemption, the cost of redemption, and the deliverance which has been afforded us by the Redeemer.

I would like to direct your attention to several passages of Scripture where different aspects of our redemption are presented to us, in order that we might rejoice in God's provided redemption and praise God for His Redeemer.

The first passage to which we direct your attention is I Peter 1:18-19: "Forasmuch as ye know that ye were not redeemed wih corruptible things, as silver and gold, from your vain conversation received by tradition from your fathers; But with the precious blood of Christ, as of a lamb without blemish and without spot." Ye were not *redeemed* with corruptible things. The word the Apostle chose to use in this text, which is translated by the English word "redeemed," is a word that emphasizes an act: it is the act of setting free, the act of liberating. The word the Apostle used here does not intimate, in itself, the price of redemption; it does not signify the need of redemption; it does not signify the destiny of the redeemed. Rather, it emphasizes that a purchase was necessary, and a purchase has been accomplished. God owns the world and all that is within creation. Because God is the Creator, all that came into being by the word of His power is rightly His. We are His by creation; therefore we are answerable to Him as creatures to the Creator. But when God would bring many sons into glory—that we should be found to the praise of the glory of His grace—God did not bring us into glory by creating us, but rather by purchasing us for Himself. When the Apostle says we were not redeemed with corruptible things but with the precious blood of Christ, he is emphasizing the fact that God who had created entered into a separate act, or work, whereby the One who already possessed us bought us to Himself that we might be doubly His: His by creation, and His by a purchased redemption.

When we turn to other passages we find that the Word of God amplifies this basic concept of an act of purchase. If you will turn with me to Revelation 5:9 we find: ". . . they sung a new song, saying, Thou art worthy to take the book, and to open the seals thereof: for thou wast slain, and hast redeemed us to God by thy blood out of every kindred, and tongue, and people, and nation." *Thou hast redeemed us to God by Thy blood!* We find a different word is used in the original text. It is the word which means "to go shopping" or "to go into the market to purchase." The Apostle John, in Revelation 5:9, emphasizes the method by which the redemption of which Peter spoke has been accomplished. It is a redemption by purchase, and the purchase price is stated—it is redemption by blood. The Apostle John uses a different word than that used by Peter, for Peter was emphasizing that God has done an act, but the Apostle John is emphasizing the method by which this act has been accomplished. We have been bought in the market by God by blood. The Apostle John is emphasizing not only the act of purchase, but the additional fact of the purchase price.

If you turn back to Peter's statement (I Peter 1:18) you will find that Peter has shown us that the redemption price was the blood of Christ: ". . . ye were not redeemed with corruptible things"—and the corruptible things he mentions are silver and gold. Silver and gold are corruptible and are corrupted because they are under the curse. When Adam sinned, the ground upon which he trod was cursed by God. God said to Adam, ". . . cursed is the ground for thy sake . . ." (Genesis 3:17), or because of his sin. All that the ground contained, then, was under the curse of God. The silver and gold were cursed by God, and an accursed thing could never be used to pay a satisfactory redemption price to God. So, the Apostle says that when we were redeemed, we were not redeemed with that which was corruptible because it was corrupted, namely, silver and gold; but that we were redeemed with the precious blood of Christ as of a Lamb without blemish and without spot. The Lamb whose blood was the purchase price was uncorruptible and uncorrputed. And the Apostle is contrasting corruptible silver with uncorruptible blood, corrupted gold with an uncorrupted Son of God. And Peter and John agreed that when God purchased us the purchasing price was none other than the blood of God's own Son.

When we turn to Galatians 3:13 we find that the Apostle writes, concerning our redemption: "Christ hath redeemed us from the curse of the law, being made a curse for us: for it is written, Cursed is every one that hangeth on a tree." In the original text the Apostle chose a compound word; it is the word we found in Revelation 5:9, "to purchase," but to that word the preposition "out of" is added. The compound word means "to purchase out of so that it can never return." This word emphasizes the result of the redemption, the result of the purchase by the blood of Christ. When we were purchased out from the curse of the law and bondage to sin we were purchased out so completely and effectively that we can never be returned to that slave market again. This would be a very precious truth for any child of God acquainted with the Roman slave system to have brought home to his own heart. A master might purchase a slave and, at will or according to his whim, he could return that slave to the slave market, put him on the auction block, and sell the slave to a new owner. A man might have a slave whom he had purchased in his younger years, one whom he had worked through the years and who was approaching old age. And when infirmity and decrepitude set in, instead of providing for that slave because of his long service, the master might return him to the slave block in order to realize a pittance out of his sale. The slave would be delivered into the hand of one who recognized his weakness and infirmity and expected to get a return for his investment as quickly as possible. Therefore, to be sold again meant that the slave would be anticipating greater rigors and greater suffering than he had endured before.

The Apostle tells us that when Christ redeemed us in a redemptive act, and purchased us for Himself by the payment of a price, He redeemed us or purchased us out of the slave market in order that we might be delivered from its bondage forever—delivered to a new slavery, a slavery to love, but delivered from slavery and bondage to sin. The Lord Himself is inferring this precious truth in John 10:28-30: "I give unto them eternal life; and they shall never perish, neither shall any man pluck them out of my hand. My Father, which gave them me, is greater than all; and no man is able to pluck them out of my Father's hand. I and my Father are one."

Christ is emphasizing the security which belongs to the child of God because he has been purchased by the Father to be given, as a love gift, to the Son; the security that is the part and the experience of the child of God, who *has been* redeemed. This purchase-out-never-to-be-returned is the basis of our confidence that that which God has purchased for Himself He will never surrender to the ownership of another.

There is a fourth word that is used in the New Testament concerning redemption. We find it in a passage such as Romans 3:24, where the Apostle writes, "Being justified freely by his grace through the redemption that is in Christ Jesus." In the original text the word translated "redemption" differs from the other three words that we referred to. This word has in view the destiny of the one who has been redeemed; it emphasizes the thoroughness and the completeness of the redemption. We have been redeemed through and through; we have been thoroughly redeemed by God. And the Apostle affirms in Romans 3:24 that we have been justified freely by His grace by the *through-and-through* redemption that is in Jesus Christ.

In Romans 8:23 the same writer says, ". . . not only they, but ourselves also, which have the firstfruits of the Spirit, even we ourselves groan within ourselves, waiting for the adoption, to wit, the redemption of our body." The body as well as the soul has been redeemed from the curse and from slavery to sin. While we live in an unredeemed body now, God has promised that our redemption will be through and through, and our redemption includes the redemption of this body. It is the future prospect that belongs to the child of God.

In I Corinthians 1:30 the Apostle, speaking of Jesus Christ, says that Christ of God "is made unto us wisdom, and righteousness, and sanctification, and redemption: That, according as it is written, He that glorieth, let him glory in the Lord." The Apostle is anticipating the completeness of our redemption when we shall be transformed into Christ's likeness—body, soul, and spirit made like unto Him. Again, in Ephesians 1:14, the Apostle tells us that the Holy Spirit is the "earnest of our inheritance until the redemption of the purchased possession [or, with the view to the redemption of the purchased possession], unto the praise of his glory."

In this last group of references, the Apostle is emphasizing that which is future. Previously, the Apostles have emphasized that which is our past experience. There has been a purchase. This purchase was by the payment of a price, and the price was blood. This purchase has freed us from the slave market once and for all, and to it we can never be returned. But this purchase has put a glorious prospect before us, the prospect of the redemption of the body, the prospect of the redemption of the total person into the likeness of Jesus Christ, because God's work of redemption will not stop short of completion. As we mount truth upon truth, we see the care which God, in His infinite wisdom, has taken that we, who were in the slave market to be auctioned off, should be purchased, not because we were of value to the Purchaser, but because the Purchaser delighted to purchase, that He might set us free. We extol the grace of God that has brought us freedom. We praise God, as the Apostle praised God, that there is liberty in Christ, and that we can stand fast in the liberty wherewith Christ has made us free. But that liberty that belongs to the children of God always rests upon redemption. It rests upon the payment of a price in order that we might be set free by the Purchaser. As long as we were in the slave market of sin, as long as we were under bondage and slavery to Satan, God had no right to touch the one who belonged to another. God could not go arbitrarily into the household of Satan to set us free. God could not set us free until first of all we had become His property, until first of all He had redeemed us. But when He had redeemed us, then He could dispose of His own property and His own possessions as it pleased Him. In order that Jesus Christ might give us freedom, and that He might deliver us from the shackles of sin, He entered into an act of purchase; He paid the purchase price, His own blood, and He set free whom He had purchased to Himself, in order that they might be brought to the destiny of those who have become members of the household of faith. The Word of God, then, would give us warrant for exalting God because of the greatness of our redemption.

But if we are to have redemption, there must be a Redeemer. In the Old Testament, God, pictorially, was preparing the way for the coming Redeemer, for He had instituted a custom in the Old Testament that graphically portrayed the work of the Lord Jesus Christ as God's Redeemer. If an Israelite was sold into bondage or delivered himself into slavery because of indebtedness, provision was made by which that indentured servant could be set free. It was through the provision we know as the kinsman-redeemer: one who was kin to the slave had the right and the responsibility to pay the price in order that his kinsman might be delivered from bondage. But there were certain stipulations laid down as to who could be the redeemer, and upon what terms this redemption of the slave could be accomplished. Briefly, may we point out to you four facts.

First, it was necessary that the one who did the work of redeeming the slave be the kinsman of the slave. Not anyone who was moved by compassion when he looked upon the plight of a slave could redeem him. That right of redemption was reserved for a kinsman. You will recall that when Ruth was to be delivered into bondage, it was the right of Boaz to deliver her because he was a kinsman. If Jesus Christ is to be a Redeemer for men Jesus Christ must be related to men, or He is not eligible to become their Redeemer. The writer to the Hebrews, cognizant of this requirement from the Old Testament, shows us how Christ met this condition so that He could be a Redeemer (2:14-15): ". . . as the children are partakers of flesh and blood, he also himself likewise took part of the same; that through death he might destroy him that had the power of death, that is, the devil; And deliver them who through fear of death were all their lifetime subject to bondage." Then the Apostle continues by showing us that Jesus Christ did not identify Himself with angels, for if He were an angel He would be ineligible to redeem men. But Jesus Christ, the eternal Son of God, through the virgin birth took upon Himself full and complete humanity in order that He, as the Son of man, related to men by a human birth, might be their representative and their kinsman-Redeemer. Jesus Christ was related to men—"He became flesh" for the work of redemption.

Second, we find from the Old Testament that it was necessary for the redeemer to have a redemption price to pay to set the slave free. He must be able to redeem. The nearest kinsman of Ruth was unable to redeem, and Boaz came forward to be the kinsman-redeemer, not only because he was related, but because he had an ability that the prior kinsman did not have: he had the substance by which he might redeem. If Jesus Christ is to become a redeemer for men, He must have a satisfactory redemption price. We find, when we turn to Acts 20:28, that Jesus Christ was One who was able to redeem, for we read that the elders are to "Take heed . . . unto yourselves, and to all the flock, over the which the Holy Ghost hath made you overseers, to feed the church of God, which he hath purchased with his own blood." His blood was His purchase price. The blood that was offered for our redemption was not blood of man alone, for it would have had finite and limited worth, but it was the blood of the eternal Son of God who had become flesh. It was blood of infinite value. It was blood that could be shed for an infinite number of sinners. It was blood which could fill a reservoir sufficient to cleanse the sin of the world. Peter reminded us of the fact (I Peter 1:18-19) that we were not redeemed with corruptible blood but with incorruptible, by none other than the blood of the Son of God who as the Lamb of God offered Himself for the sins of the world.

The third requirement of the kinsman-redeemer was that he must be willing to redeem. The one who was the nearest kinsman to Ruth was not willing to assume responsibility for Ruth after he had redeemed her. Therefore, he must forego his right as a kinsman-redeemer. Boaz was not only related, not only able, but he was willing to redeem. We follow our Lord into the Garden of Gethsemane and we listen as He poured out His heart to God in prayer and cried, ". . . if thou be willing, remove this cup from me: nevertheless not my will, but thine, be done" (Luke 22:42). We recognize that He was signifying He was not only able but willing. It is testified of Him in Hebrews 10:7: "I come . . . to do thy will. . . ."

When Peter sought to dissuade Christ from going to the cross, Peter was reproached by Christ who said, "Get thee behind me, Satan: . . . for thou savourest not the things that be of God . . ." (Matthew 16:23). When Peter sought to protect Christ from those who would lay hand on Him to drag Him before a Roman tribunal, Peter's sword was returned to its sheath, for our Lord reminded Peter that He could call upon God for ten legions of angels who could deliver Him from the adversaries. But He went with the Romans because He was willing.

If Jesus Christ had been an unwilling sacrifice, God would have perpetrated the greatest crime ever committed in the history of the universe. But if Jesus Christ was a willing sacrifice, the cross of Christ stands as the greatest demonstration of submission and obedience to the will of God that the world has ever seen. He was willing to redeem.

And finally, it was necessary that the redeemer should not himself need the redemption which he purposes to provide for another. This was to say, no slave could redeem another slave, for if a man were in bondage to another he was in no position to redeem someone else. His need was as great as the need of any other slave. If Jesus Christ was to redeem men from the slave market of sin, He must be without sin Himself. That is why it is significant that the writer to the Hebrews (4:15) says, ". . . we have not an high priest which cannot be touched with the feeling of our infirmities; but was in all points tempted like as we are, yet without sin." The same writer who said that we were redeemed with the precious blood of Christ also said (I Peter 2:22-24) that Christ "did no sin, neither was guile found in his mouth: Who, when he was reviled, reviled not again; when he suffered, he threatened not; but committed himself to him that judgeth righteously: Who his own self bare our sins in his own body on the tree, that we, being dead to sins, should live unto righteousness: by whose stripes ye were healed." The Word of God presents the truth that Jesus Christ was an acceptable Redeemer for the human race, for sin had not laid its finger upon Him. He, as the sinless One, needed no redemption for Himself but He could offer His blood as the purchase price for sinners everywhere. We can extol God, not only for the redemption that is in Christ, but also for the Redeemer, the One who took upon Himself flesh, that He might redeem us; the One who was able to redeem because of His infinite Person; the One who was willing to redeem because He submitted Himself to the will of God; the One who, because He was not implicated in sin, could offer Himself as a sacrifice for the sins of the world.

This Redeemer has made a purchase; it is a purchase by His own blood, a purchase that sets us free and promises that we will never be brought back into slavery again. It is a purchase that sets glory as our destiny, and security as our confidence and assurance, because of the redemption that is in Christ Jesus. If you should be without Christ as your Redeemer, may we say to you, on the authority of the

Word of God, that it is not by works of righteousness which we have done, but according to His mercy He has saved us—not by works, but by purchase. Have you become His purchased possession by faith in Christ?

8 ◆ Reconciliation

II Corinthians 5:14-21

WHILE WALKING DOWN Main Street one day recently, I glanced at my watch and realized that it had stopped; I had forgotten to wind it. I set it by guess. Passing one of the large jewelry stores, I noticed that a chronometer was prominently displayed, and I set my watch to conform to the time indicated on the chronometer. While I was setting my watch I was conscious that a man had stopped and was looking at the same timepiece that I was setting my watch by. I could see that with a great deal of pride he was checking a brand-new wristwatch. He looked at the chronometer and then looked at his watch. I heard him mutter, "It's a minute off." He adjusted his watch so that it conformed to the chronometer and proceeded on his way.

A few doors down the street was another jewelry store. There, too, a chronometer was prominently displayed. When the man got to that chronometer he stopped and looked at his watch again. Then he began to frown because the two chronometers were not synchronized and each gave a different time. The poor fellow did not know what to do—whether to accept the setting indicated by the first jewelry store, or to change his watch again to conform to this second jewelry store. I watched to see what he would do. I saw him turn, and cross the street, and make his way to a third jewelry store where a third chronometer was displayed. I did not have the nerve to follow him across the street, but I presume he was taking an average of the three, and setting his watch accordingly. That man was reconciling his watch, bringing it into conformity to a standard.

We sit down at least once a month and reconcile the bank account. At the end of the month there has to be a reckoning, a reconciling, when the figures in your bankbook are brought to conform to the figures furnished you by the bank. When you adjust your balance to conform to the statement furnished you by the bank, in the Biblical sense of the word you are *reconciling* your account. What I am trying to show you is that the word which puzzles so many of God's children because it seems to be such a complex and complicated theological word is basically very simple. The word "reconciliation" in the Scriptures means "to cause to conform to a standard, to be adjusted to a specified standard."

According to the Word of God, the world is out of balance. The world does not conform to the standard which God has set. This is pictured for us very graphically in Romans 5:6 where the Apostle presents many details concerning the doctrine of reconciliation. We read: ". . . when we were yet without strength, in due time Christ died for the ungodly." There are two statements in that verse which emphasize the fact that we do not conform to a divine standard. Paul says, first, "We were without strength," and second, "We were ungodly." The phrase "without strength" emphasizes our weakness, our total, complete inability to render ourselves acceptable to God or to conform to God's standard. Even though we knew what God required, we were unable to conform ourselves to that requirement because we were without strength. But Paul says, in the second place, that we were ungodly. He emphasizes the fact that we do not conform. Not only are we without the ability to conform, but we actually do not conform to the standards that God has set.

Paul continues: "For scarcely for a righteous man will one die: yet peradventure for a good man some would even dare to die. But God commendeth his love toward us, in that, while we were yet sinners, Christ died for us" (vv. 7-8). There we have the third evidence that we do not conform to God's standards, for Paul says that we were sinners. The Apostle was emphasizing not only the nature which controls us, but also the products of that nature. We not only were impotent and unable to conform to God's standards; we were not only ungodly, because God was left out of our concept; but further, we practiced ungodliness and unrighteousness, so that God characterized us as sinners in His sight.

Paul continues: "Much more then, being now justified by his blood, we shall be saved from wrath through him" (v. 9). This gives us the fourth evidence that we do not conform to God's standards: far from being objects of divine favor, we are objects of divine wrath. God passed a sentence upon all who were weak, and all who were ungodly, and all who were sinners, and the divine judgment upon sin is divine wrath, so that we were the objects of divine wrath. But further, Paul says, ". . . if, when we were enemies, we were reconciled to God by the death of his Son, much more, being reconciled, we shall be saved by his life" (v. 10). Paul says that we were enemies; this emphasizes the fact that our ungodliness, and our ignorance, and our weakness, and our sin were translated into overt acts of warfare and rebellion against God. We were not placid in our ignorance and weakness; we were not passive in our sin and ungodliness; but we were virulently active, so that Paul says, "We were enemies." Because of these reasons which Paul presents in this brief passage, we have to confess that we did not conform to God's standards any more than a watch which is left unwound conforms to the chronometer. Because of what we were by nature, there was need that we should be brought to conform to God's standard.

It is very important that we should realize that God Himself is the standard by which He tests men. God has not set up a standard apart from Himself, from which He is detached and to which He asks men to conform. But God Himself is the unalterable, unchangeable standard by which men are tested. And it is because men have sinned and fallen short of the glory of God that there is need for reconciliation. That is why, in Romans 3, Paul emphasizes the fact that *all* have sinned and come short of the glory of God. When Paul says that they have come short, he is emphasizing the great need for reconciliation, the great need to be made to conform, or to be adjusted to the divine standard. I am sure we have heard of the rather amusing story of the factory that every morning telephoned a bureau for the time and set their clocks to conform to that information. When the noon whistle of the factory blew, the head of the bureau changed his clock to conform to the noon whistle. It was no wonder they were in endless confusion when each was accepting the other as the norm and adjusting their clocks accordingly. If we have a flexible standard, then all need for reconciliation disappears, for every man becomes a standard within himself, and there can be no change to conform to a standard unless the standard is absolute and inflexible. And when man would be certain in fixing time, he causes all of his timepieces to be adjusted to the heavenly bodies, because they are the most unchanging and inflexible standards that we know anything about. God sets His holiness as that inflexible standard by which men are tested and it becomes the standard to which men are caused to be conformed.

The words of a well-known hymn erroneously state, "God is reconciled." What does that suggest? That God needed to be conformed to a standard; that God somehow was out of harmony, out of conformity to the accepted norm, and that God has been changed so as to conform? This an utter impossibility! We must correctly sing, "To God *I'm* reconciled," for in the Scriptural teaching on reconciliation God is always the Reconciler and man is always the one who is reconciled to God. God brings us to Himself and causes us to be adjusted to His standards.

As we consider the Scriptural teaching on reconciliation, we want to emphasize, first of all, the fact that God has reconciled the world to Himself. Will you read what the Apostle Paul writes in II Corinthians 5:19: ". . . God was in Christ, reconciling the world unto himself, not imputing their trespasses unto them. . . ." Note: God was in Christ *reconciling the world.* Now the word "world" does not refer to the inhabited earth—that is, this globe on which we live—but rather to the world of those who, according to Romans 5, were called weak and ungodly and sinners and enemies and who were under wrath. God has so changed the relationship of the world to Himself that God can conform the world to His standards. Now, be very clear in your thinking—this does not mean that God has saved all men, nor that all men are now saved, nor that all men ultimately will be saved. Such a teaching would contradict a great body of teaching of the Word of God. Rather, this emphasizes the fact that the Lord Jesus Christ has laid a foundation upon which God may take His stand to reach out to sinners and bring them to Himself. God could not arbitrarily bridge the gulf between Himself and sinful men. There must be some basis upon which divine grace exercises itself, and manifests itself. God, in Christ Jesus, was changing the relationship of the world to Himself so that men in the world are now savable.

When God created Adam and Eve and placed them in the Garden of Eden, Adam and God enjoyed a face-to-face fellowship, the one to the other. It was God's custom to come into the Garden, as

Genesis 3 tells us, in the cool of the day in order that He might walk and talk with Adam and Eve, so that they might enjoy sweet fellowship and companionship together. We do not know how long this state continued, but we have the record given to us in Genesis 3 that that state was interrupted by the disobedience of Adam and Eve. Adam and Eve deliberately and willfully turned their backs upon God. Consequently, fellowship between God and Adam was not possible because God was a holy God and Adam was now a sinner. Adam was weak, Adam was ungodly, Adam was at enmity with God, and Adam was under wrath. God had to turn His back upon Adam because He could not continue in fellowship with an unholy creature. The privilege of face-to-face fellowship was totally and completely lost.

Warfare exists on the part of man against God. That was the state into which the world was plunged because of Adam's sin, and the world remained in that state until Jesus Christ came to reconcile the world to God. Jesus Christ made a covering over for the sin of the world, and when Jesus Christ covered over, or made a propitiation for the sin of the world, God could turn His face manward. And God, who had had to turn His back upon sinners because there was no basis upon which He might receive sinners, could turn His face toward man and could stretch out His hands toward men and say, "Come unto Me." The death of Jesus Christ gave God the basis for receiving men to Himself. God was not reconciled to the world, but the world was reconciled to God. It was because of the death of Christ that the world was brought into this relationship to God— the world was rendered savable.

A second fact concerning this doctrine of reconciliation is emphasized in the Scriptures. Not only was the world reconciled to God, but according to II Corinthians 5:20 there is reconciliation of the individual to God. The reconciliation of the world to God made possible the reconciliation of the individual to God. In II Corinthians 5:20 we read, "Now then we are ambassadors for Christ, as though God did beseech you by us: we pray you in Christ's stead, be ye reconciled to God." Whereas the death of Christ brought God into relationship to the world, man still is out of relationship to God and needs to be brought back into an intimacy of fellowship with God. Paul teaches us that the world has been reconciled to God. God's face is toward the world, inviting the world to Himself, but individuals in the world have their backs to God. They need to respond to God's invitation to be reconciled to God, to be adjusted to His standards, to be conformed to Him through Jesus Christ. This is the reconciliation of the individual to God.

The Word of God has a good deal to say concerning the basis of these two aspects of reconciliation. Thus, in the third place, we must consider the Scriptural teaching on the basis by which the world was reconciled to God, and sinners individually may be reconciled to God. Notice that this reconciliation is through Christ. Look at it in II Corinthians 5:18: ". . . all things are of God, who hath reconciled us to himself by Jesus Christ. . . ." Reconciliation of the world, and of the individual, is by Jesus Christ. In Romans 5:11 this same fact is presented: "And not only so, but we also joy in God through our Lord Jesus Christ, by whom we have now received the atonement," or, as it is literally, ". . . we have received the reconciliation." Thus we see that the work of God in reconciling the world and sinners to Himself is through His Son, the Lord Jesus Christ.

In the second place, Paul shows us that reconciliation is accomplished through Christ's death, for he says (Romans 5:10), ". . . if, when we were enemies, we were reconciled to God by the death of his Son. . . ." Reconciliation depended not only upon Christ but, further, upon the death of Christ. It was Christ's death that reconciled the world to God, and made it possible for individual sinners to be reconciled to God.

In Ephesians 2:16, the Apostle points out that, in the third place, we were reconciled by the cross, ". . . that he might reconcile both unto God in one body by the cross, having slain the enmity thereby." In Ephesians 2 the Apostle is speaking of Jew and Gentile, who, through the cross of Christ, are brought to conformity to God, and it is the cross of Christ that reconciles Jew and Gentile to God the Father. We are reconciled by the cross.

In the fourth place, we were reconciled by blood: ". . . not only so, but we also joy in God through out Lord Jesus Christ, by whom we have now received the atonement [reconciliation]" (Romans 5:11). The word translated "reconciliation," or "atonement," is the word used in the Old Testament in regard to applying blood to the Mercy Seat. When the high priest caught the blood of the sacrificed animal in the basin, and carried that basin in through the Holy place, behind the veil, and into the presence of God in the Holy of Holies, He sprinkled that blood upon the Mercy Seat. He was then making reconciliation for the sins of the people; and reconciliation, in the Old Testament, was always by the sprinkling of blood. Apart from blood there was no reconciliation. One could not be changed to meet God's standard apart from the shedding of blood. When, in Romans 5:11, Paul says, ". . . we have now received the reconciliation [or the atonement]," he is reminding us of that which every slain lamb in the Old Testament taught—that apart from the shedding of blood there could be no remission of sins, and apart from blood sacrifice the world could not be reconciled to God, and sinners could not be reconciled to a holy and righteous God.

Finally, in the fifth place, we find that reconciliation is based upon Christ's identification with sinners so that He took their place. In II Corinthians 5:20-21 we read, "Now then we are ambassadors for Christ, as though God did beseech you by us: we pray you in Christ's stead, be ye reconciled to God. For he hath made him to be sin for us, who knew no sin; that we might be made the righteousness of God in him." When the Apostle uses the word translated "for" in verse 21 he is giving us an explanation as to how reconciliation is possible. You can be adjusted to God's standard, because God made Christ to become sin for us. The One who knew no sin, the One in whose lips had never been found guile, took upon Himself our sin in order that He might bear our sins to the cross and offer Himself as an acceptable substitute to God for us—on our behalf, in our place. And when Jesus Christ identified Himself with sinners and went to the cross on their behalf and in their place, He was making possible the doctrine of reconciliation. He was making it possible for God to conform the world to Himself, to adjust the world to His standard so that sinners in the world might find salvation because "Jesus paid it all." You can be adjusted to God, to God's standard, through Christ, by His death, by His cross, by His blood, and by His identification with sinners.

The Lord Jesus Christ in His death on the cross accomplished a great change. It was a positional change: the relationship of the world to God was changed, and the world was rendered savable. But Jesus Christ in His death on the cross also made possible a second great change, and that is not positional; it is experimental: the change of the worldling to God. That is why the Apostle, in writing to the Corinthians, emphasized that which we would call to your attention now in our consideration of this doctrine of reconciliation.

The child of God has been entrusted with a message, the message of reconciliation. Read Paul's words in II Corinthians 5:18-20: ". . . all things are of God, who hath reconciled us to himself by Jesus Christ [and now, note], and hath given to us the ministry of reconciliation; To wit, that God was in Christ, reconciling the world unto himself, not imputing their trespasses unto them; and [notice] hath committed unto us the word of reconciliation. Now then we are ambassadors for Christ, as though God did beseech you by us: we pray you in Christ's stead, be ye reconciled to God." God has reconciled the world to Himself, so that the world is rendered savable. God invites sinners to be reconciled to God through Christ in His death, and His cross, and His blood, and His identification with men. But apart from a ministry of reconciliation, those for whom reconciliation has been provided will never be adjusted to God's standard. That is why Paul says that God has committed to every child of God the ministry of telling men that God has been propitiated, God has been satisfied, God's holy and righteous demands have been met by Jesus Christ, and sinners can come to God through Christ. God has made us His ambassadors.

We have very vague ideas as to what an ambassador is. We somehow feel that an ambassador of the United States is a representative of the United States, or a representative of Congress, or a representative of the people of the United States, or a representative of the State Department. Actually an ambassador is the personal representative of the President of the United States; an ambassador represents one who is not personally present. The Apostle says that God has made us His ambassadors. Since He is not visibly present to announce the good news of reconciliation of sinners to God, God has appointed His personal representatives. Every child of God is a personal representative of the Lord Jesus Christ, and to every believer has been committed this ministry. We are to tell men that they may be conformed to God's standard; they may be reconciled to God through Jesus Christ.

God did not commit the ministry of reconciliation to angels, although angels would delight to preach the gospel if God gave them voices that human ears could hear. God committed to us, to believers, the ministry of reconciliation. The one who occupies the pulpit does not have one bit more responsibility in the ministry of reconciliation than the child of God who sits in the pew, for the Scripture says that God has committed to *us* the ministry of reconciliation. Our ministry is not primarily to tell men that they need to be reconciled to God. Men know that; they know that they are ungodly, and weak, and enemies, and sinners. Men need to know *how* they can be reconciled to God. Our ministry is the ministry of pointing to the Lord Jesus Christ, God's Agent in reconciliation, in order that men might be reconciled to God through Jesus Christ.

A life that is lived under the control of the Spirit of God, and lips that speak forth the praises of the Son of God, and the Word of God which presents Jesus Christ as the One who reconciles men to God, may all be used in the discharge of this ministry. When we stand before the judgment seat of Christ to be examined for the stewardship committed to us, we will be examined concerning our faithfulness in the ministry of telling men how they can be reconciled to God. This is not a ministry which we may take or leave; this is not an elective course. It is a ministry, an obligation divinely placed upon every child of God. The question is not, "Am I an ambassador of Jesus Christ?"; the question is, "What kind of an ambassador of Jesus Christ am I?" What is your response to the facts of the gospel of reconciliation? Are you faithful or faithless?

We have an unchanging God. That unchanging God demands that every created thing be conformed to Him. Men will either receive His reconciliation through Christ, or they will receive His judgment and separation from Him forever. An inflexible and unchanging God with an unchanging standard says, "Be reconciled to me through Christ, or be banished forever." It is that which gives importance to our ministry. Men are lost without Christ. Child of God, may the Spirit of God bring to your consciousness the fact that you have been made a minister of reconciliation. You will be examined at the judgment seat of Christ as to your faithfulness to that ministry. May God make us faithful ambassadors.

If you are without Christ, may the Spirit of God bring to your consciousness the conviction that you, as an enemy of God, do not meet God's standard. You are weak and impotent and helpless to conform yourself to God's standard. But Christ will reconcile you to God, if you by faith accept Him as your personal Saviour. Will you do that now?

9 ⟡ Propitiation

I John 2:1-10

THE CONCEPT OF god universally held by all the heathen is of a god who is angry and must be placated before any blessing can be expected from him. And all heathen religions seek to change the attitude of their god toward man so that they may receive kindnesses and mercies from his hands. It is only in the Word of God that we have pictured for us the true character of God—a God of love, a God of mercy, a God of grace, a God who, even though He must punish sinners because He is a holy God, loves sinners and seeks to pour forth mercy and grace upon sinners if a way can be found to turn loose the torrent of His love toward them.

In I Kings 18 we have pictured so graphically that which is the heathen concept of a god—a god who needs to be propitiated, who needs to have his attitude toward men completely changed so that they may gain some favor from him. In this chapter, you will recall, the Prophet Elijah is in contest with the prophets of Baal. He has challenged these prophets to a contest to demonstrate which god is the true God. We read in verses 25-26: "Elijah said unto the prophets of Baal, Choose you one bullock for yourselves, and dress it first; for ye are many; and call on the name of your gods, but put no fire under. And they took the bullock which was given them, and they dressed it, and called on the name of Baal from morning even until noon, saying, O Baal, hear us." These prophets of a false deity were trying to change their god's attitude toward them by prayer and supplication. But as a result, ". . . there was no voice, nor any that answered. And they leaped upon the altar which they made" (v. 26). Through their outward demonstrations they were seeking to change the attitude of their god from animosity and hatred to kindness and mercy. "And it came to pass at noon, that Elijah mocked them, and said, Cry aloud: for he is a god; either he is talking, or he is pursuing, or he is in a journey, or peradventure he sleepeth, and must be awaked" (v. 27). Elijah was voicing the heathen concept that a god was indifferent to the need of men, and that it took some great work on the part of man to arouse any interest, or compassion, or concern for men in a god. But we read, ". . . they cried aloud, and cut themselves after their manner with knives and lancets, till the blood gushed out upon them" (v. 28). Through personal sacrifice, suffering, and penance they were seeking to change the attitude of their god and turn his stony silence so as to receive some mercy from him.

In contrast, Elijah came before his God, not with prayers, not with outward demonstrations, not with inveterate crying, not with penance which he himself offered, but with a sacrifice. In simple faith he offered up a lamb to God. God heard, and God answered Elijah.

In this record we have vividly portrayed a common concept of God—namely, that God is hard, cold, stubborn, disinterested, and unconcerned; and it is only through prayers, through penance, and through personal sacrifice that His attitude toward sinners can be changed. When we turn to the concept of God given to us in the Word of God and revealed in the Person of Jesus Christ, we find that God, contrary to that heathen concept, is a God of infinite love, of infinite mercy, of infinite grace—a God who is concerned with the needs of His creatures, even though they be sinners; a God who has moved to meet their needs; a God who delights to pour love and mercy and grace upon them. It is not God's attitude which needs to be changed, but the great reservoir of God's love and mercy and grace needs to be poured forth, to be unloosed so that men might have their needs met in and through His gracious provision in Jesus Christ.

When we come to the Scriptural teaching on propitiation, we are studying one of the three great doctrinal words which are employed in the Scriptures to reveal to us the extent of the value of the death of Christ for the sinner. So vast is the work of Christ for sinful men that all of the benefits of Christ's death cannot be conveyed in one word, or in one line of teaching. Rather, all of the facets of the work of Christ must be examined and must be taken in conjunction so that we may see the infinite scope of the value of His death. When we studied the doctrine of redemption, we saw that redemption was the sinward aspect of the death of Christ in which Jesus Christ, by His death, purchased out of the slave market of sin those who were shackled and bound. When we studied the doctrine of reconciliation, we saw that reconciliation was the manward aspect of the death of Christ. Sinners who were separated from God by a great gulf have now been made nigh. When we come to consider this third great doctrinal word, *propitiation,* we were studying the God-ward aspect of the value of the death of Christ. While redemption was sinward, and reconciliation was manward, propitiation gives to us the third, or the God-ward aspect of the value of Christ's death for us.

Propitiation does not suggest that God needs to be changed, for our God is an unchanging God. The Father, no less than the Son, is the same yesterday, today, and forever. When the Apostle John wrote that God is love, he was not suggesting that God had begun to love after Jesus Christ had died for the sins of the world, but rather that God, eternally and infinitely, was a God of love. But the love of God for sinners could not be unloosed, could not be poured forth upon them until there was some basis upon which God might deal with men. And propitiation is the work of Christ that satisfies all the claims of divine holiness, righteousness, and justice, so that God is free to act on behalf of sinners. May we emphasize again that propitiation does not change the attitude of God; but propitiation does free God to act on behalf of sinners.

In the Old Testament we have portrayed for us in type the value of the death of Christ as that which propitiates, or releases God's love and mercy towards sinners. This propitiation is described for us in Leviticus 16, where we have God's revelation concerning the day of atonement. There are several facts about the ritual of the day of atonement that I would like to call to your attention, and which anticipate the propitiating work of Jesus Christ.

God spoke unto Moses, and in Leviticus 16:2 said, "Speak unto Aaron thy brother, that he come not at all times into the holy place within the veil before the mercy seat, which is upon the ark; that he die not: for I will appear in the cloud upon the mercy seat." The first great fact we discover is that a holy God is unapproachable because of the sinfulness of man. Moses and Aaron were not permitted to come into the presence of God except through the blood of sacrifice, and then only when they followed a prescribed ritual. God erected the outer veil and the inner veil in the Tabernacle to remind the nation Israel, and to remind us, that while God is a God of infinite love, mercy, and grace, the barrier of sin separates God from man, so that man in his sin cannot come to God.

In Leviticus 16:16-17, concerning the sprinkling of the blood, we read, ". . . he shall make an atonement [or a covering] for the holy place, because of the uncleanness of the children of Israel, and because of their transgressions in all their sins: and so shall he do for the tabernacle of the congregation, that remaineth among them in the midst of their uncleanness. And there shall be no man in the tabernacle of the congregation when he goeth in to make an atonement in the holy place. . . ." We discover from these verses that atonement, or propitiation, was necessary because of the sinfulness of the nation as represented by the priests. These verses reveal the first great fact that propitiation is necessary because God is a holy God and men are sinners. Men need to be reconciled to God; God does not need to be reconciled to men. God needs only to have a basis on which He may receive sinners. Propitiation provides this basis.

When we turn to verse 14 we discover that it is blood that does the work of propitiation. We read there that "he shall take of the blood of the bullock, and sprinkle it with his finger upon the mercy seat eastward; and before the mercy seat shall he sprinkle of the blood with his finger seven times." It was not incense which propitiated. It was not an offering of gold or silver which propitiated. It was not the prayers offered by the priest for forgiveness of the people of Israel which propitiated. It was not good works which propitiated. But is was blood which propitiated.

God appointed the place where the blood of propitiation was to be applied. The place of propitiation was the Mercy Seat above the Ark. Within the Ark was the Law which had been broken. God commanded the blood to be applied to the Mercy Seat so that the God who must be propitiated could look upon the broken Law contained in the Ark and He could be merciful to men. After the blood was applied and God was propitiated, God warded off judgment upon the sins of the nation of Israel for another twelve-month period. The writer to the Hebrews tells us (10:3) that each year when the high priest sprinkled the blood which propitiated upon the Mercy Seat, the place of propitiation, there was a remembrance made again of sin. Each time the sacrifice was offered and the blood of propitiation was applied, it was a recognition of obligation. The children of Israel were renewing an indebtedness, and each year on the day of atonement they offered the blood in order that the note might be deferred, for it was impossible, the writer to the Hebrews tells us, that the blood of bulls and goats could finally take away sin.

All this anticipated the Lord Jesus Christ, "Whom God hath set forth to be a propitiation through faith in his blood, to declare his righteousness for the remission of sins that are past, through the forbearance of God" (Romans 3:25). What the Apostle is telling us is that when Jesus Christ went to the cross, He gathered together all those notes of indebtedness which the nation Israel had renewed every year on the day of atonement, and He, by the offering up of His blood as that which propitiated a holy God, made a final and complete settlement for all of those notes. As a result there was remission, there was forgiveness of sins that are past.

From the Old Testament, then, we discover the basic facts that God is the One who must be propitiated. God needs to be propitiated because of the sins of man, and it is only blood that can propitiate. God has appointed a place of propitiation, and when the propitiating blood is applied at the place of propitiation, God is rendered propitious, and God can manifest His grace and His mercy and His love because He has found a way whereby He can let all His love and mercy pour forth to a sinner. Yet the propitiation provided in the Old Testament was temporary.

When we come over to the New Testament we find that the same basic truths which the Old Testament presented in the ritual of the day of atonement are finally and completely fulfilled by the Lord Jesus Christ. If you turn, for instance, to Hebrews 9:28 you discover there that propitiation was offered to God because men were sinners: "So Christ was once offered to bear the sins of many. . . ." When Jesus Christ went to the cross, He bore our sins on Him there. Peter tells us that He bore "our sins in his own body on the tree . . ." (I, 2:24) . The Prophet Isaiah, anticipating this One, said that "All we like sheep have gone astray; we have turned every one to his own way; and the Lord hath laid on him the iniquity of us all" (53:6). It was sin that sent Jesus Christ to Calvary. Just as it was sin in the nation Israel that caused an animal to be offered on the day of atonement, so it was sin in the human race that caused Christ to be offered as a sacrifice on the cross.

We discover, in the second place, that when Jesus Christ went to offer Himself as the sacrifice for sins, the One to whom He offered Himself was God. Read the words in Hebrews 9:13-14: "For if the blood of bulls and of goats, and the ashes of an heifer sprinkling the unclean, sanctifieth to the purifying of the flesh: How much more shall the blood of Christ, who through the eternal Spirit offered himself without spot to God, purge your conscience from dead works to serve the living God?" Observe in this connection that the Apostle says that Christ offered Himself without spot *to God*. Jesus Christ recognized the fact that God the Father had within Him a well of mercy and grace to dispense to men in their misery and need, but that mercy could not be poured forth until a basis had been found by which God might be just and at the same time justify the ungodly. Jesus Christ recognized that God must be satisfied before sinners could be redeemed. Therefore, Jesus Christ offered Himself without spot to God so that He might propitiate God.

We find, in the third place, that Jesus Christ offered to God that which could make a propitiation, for in the same Hebrews 9:14 we read, "How much more shall the blood of Christ . . . purge your conscience from dead works to serve the living God?" That which propitiated was *His own blood*. In Hebrews 9:22 the Apostle says, ". . . almost all things are by the law purged with blood; and without shedding of blood is no remission." Because there was no propitiation, no forgiveness, no reconciliation apart from the shedding of blood, Jesus Christ offered His blood as that which would propitiate God, so that God through the blood of Christ might have a basis upon which He could extend His hand to sinners and invite them to Himself through His Son who made propitiation for them.

When we turn to I John 2:2 we discover the One who made propitiation. In the Old Testament it was a goat whose blood was sprinkled by a human priest upon the Mercy Seat, but in the New Testament it was not the blood of an animal, for animal blood had only transitory and temporary value. It was the blood of the Son offered by the eternal Son of God who made propitiation for us. And so, the Apostle John writes, ". . . he is the propitiation for our sins: and not for ours only, but also for the sins of the whole world." And in I John 4:10: "Herein is love, not that we loved God, but that he loved us, and sent his Son to be the propitiation for our sins." Or you may read it this way: "He loved us and sent His Son to be the One who does the propitiating, by offering the propitiating blood upon the place of propitiation."

Further, we discover an additional fact. It was the body of Jesus Christ which became the place of propitiation. The Mercy Seat was the place where the blood was sprinkled in the Old Testament, but at Calvary the body of the Lord Jesus Christ, who hung upon the cross, became the place where propitiation was made. Peter referred to this fact when he said, "Who his own self bare our sins in his own body on the tree, that we, being dead to sins, should live unto righteousness: by whose stripes ye were healed" (I, 2:24). Notice the phrase, "in his own body." When the Lord Jesus Christ went to Calvary's cross, He went there to pour out His life's blood. He was offering a propitiatory sacrifice to God. He was doing the work of propitiating God. His blood was that which propitiated, and His body, offered on the cross, was the place where that propitiation was made. He, in effect, was saying to God, "I am what the Mercy Seat was in Israel. My body is the place where all of the broken Law is gathered together, and where all of the indebtedness is accumulated. My body is the place where propitiation will be made." Then He poured out His blood as a propitiatory sacrifice to God, and He lifted His voice and prayed, "Father, forgive them." He recognized the indebtedness of the sinner; He recognized that God was the One who needed to be propitiated. He offered His blood to God so that God might be propitiated, and there might be a basis upon which God could remove judgment for all who come to God through Jesus Christ.

As we see Jesus Christ offering propitiation to God, there are several facts that stand out unmistakably. Jesus Christ propitiated *the Father*. Jesus Christ, and Jesus Christ alone, was the One who could offer Himself so that God, who had to deal in judgment for sin because He is a holy God, could pour forth His mercy, love, and grace upon sinners. Christ is *the One who propitiated*. Christ, as He hung upon the cross, was *the place* where that propitiation was made. Not upon any earthly altar, not in any man-made building, not through any man-devised sacrifice, or penance, or prayer, but in His own body He made propitiation. Christ's blood was *that which propitiated,* and the sinner receives the benefits of a propitiation. And God, who had had to say to the sinner, "Between us there is a great gulf fixed," could now say, "Jesus Christ, in His own body on the tree, has borne your sins. There is a gulf, but there is a bridge over the gulf, and I have found a way whereby I might be just and the Justifier of the one who does no more than believe. I have found a way by which My eternal love and mercy and grace and compassion might be poured out upon sinners who come to Me because I am a propitiated God."

In Luke 18 our Lord related an incident which revealed a precious truth concerning this doctrine. In the parable concerning those who trusted that they were righteous, our Lord said (v. 10), "Two men went up into the temple to pray; the one a Pharisee, and the other a publican." The Pharisee, trusting his own righteousness, felt that God's attitude toward him could be changed by his prayer, by his offerings, by his conduct, by his deeds. By reminding God of what he was, he hoped to change the attitude of God toward sinners. And so he stood and prayed, "God, I thank thee, that I am not as other men are, extortioners, unjust, adulterers, or even as this publican. I fast twice in the week, I give tithes of all that I possess" (vv. 11-12). This man thought he was acceptable to God—first of all, because he was better than other men, and second, because of the things he did in God's name: he tithed, he prayed, he fasted. He hoped that God would receive him because of this.

On the other hand, the publican stood and prayed, saying, "God be merciful to me a sinner" (v. 13); or, to read this literally, "God, be propitiated to me, a sinner." What he was saying was: "God, I confess my guilt. I have broken the Law. You are the One against whom I have sinned. To You I am responsible. I am a sinner; You are a holy God. I am putting myself under the blood of the goat, which sprinkles the mercy seat. I am putting myself under that protective blood. Now God, let Your attitude toward me be your attitude toward sin that is covered by blood." He did not deny his sin and his guilt; he did not offer something to God that came from his own hands; but he asked God to manifest mercy toward him on the basis of the blood that had been shed as required, according to

Leviticus 16. And Christ said, ". . . this man went down to his house justified rather than the other . . ." (v. 14). Why? Because he put himself under the blood which gave God a basis for dealing with him in mercy and in grace.

I submit to you, on the authority of the Word of God, that God must deal with you in judgment because He is a holy, a righteous, and a just God—unless a way is found whereby God might be propitiated. You have nothing you can offer to God to satisfy Him, other than the propitiating blood of the Lord Jesus Christ. We need not pray as this publican prayed, "God be merciful to me, a sinner," for God is merciful. God has manifested His grace and mercy in giving Christ to be a propitiatory sacrifice. We, like the publican, come and put ourselves under the propitiating blood. We claim the fact that God is a propitious God, and putting ourselves under the propitiating blood we accept His forgiveness because He is a God who has been propitiated by the propitiatory sacrifice, and the propitiating blood of His Son.

Israel, in the Old Testament, looked to the Mercy Seat as the place where sinful men could meet a gracious God. We look to the Lord Jesus Christ crucified on Calvary, and recognize that He bore our sins in His body on the tree. He is our place of propitiation. We behold His blood shed for the sins of the world, and recognize that it is His blood that propitiates. We see ourselves in our sin, and confess our need of redemption and reconciliation; but we look through Christ to a God who has been satisfied with the death of His Son, a God who has been propitiated, and a God who can let His love flow forth because Christ has made a propitiation for the sins of the world.

What do you have to offer God to render yourself acceptable to Him? Could it be that you, like the priests of Baal, are trying through your prayers, through an outward demonstration, through penance, through sacrifice, through suffering, to win God's forgiveness or God's love? May I point you to Jesus Christ, the One who is our Mercy Seat; to His blood which propitiates; and to the God and Father of our Lord Jesus Christ who is willing and able to receive any sinner who will come to Him, for He is a propitious God.

10 ❖ Justification

Romans 3:21—4:8

IT IS A principle in most Western courts of law that a sentence in any case must be in accordance with the facts presented. No judge has the right to clear the guilty or to condemn the innocent; and if justice is to be served, the judgment by the judge must be in keeping with this principle. In the Old Testament this principle is laid down very clearly in respect to the administration of justice in the nation Israel. In Deuteronomy 25:1 it is written, "If there be a controversy between men, and they come unto judgment, that the judges may judge them; then they shall justify the righteous, and condemn the wicked." This verse might be translated, "They shall acquit the righteous and condemn the wicked." In order that justice should be served, the Mosaic Law required that every sentence should be in accord with this principle. It is because of this principle that Justice has always been pictured as being blindfolded, so that judgment should be according to truth and not with respect to persons.

This which is a principle of law to regulate affairs among men is also a principle by which God must administer justice. When God, as a holy and righteous Judge, sits in judgment upon men, His judgment must be in accordance with truth and righteousness. God must justify the righteous and condemn the wicked. No judge could administer justice who treated facts other than as they are; and a judge would be an unjust judge if, out of favoritism, he cleared the guilty or condemned the righteous. This law is so inflexible that it has given rise to what might well be called "the greatest riddle ever faced," the riddle which God faced when, as a holy and righteous

God, He sought to accept sinners into His presence. How could God be just and at the same time justify the ungodly?

The Apostle Paul has stated the problem in Romans 3:26. How could God "be just, and the justifier of him which believeth in Jesus"? The Apostle, in verse 23, had summarized the teaching of the first three chapters of Romans as he gave the divine verdict: ". . . all have sinned, and come short of the glory of God." This states the universality of sin, the experience of the human race in sin. *All have sinned.* Therefore, when God, a just and righteous God, sits in judgment in order to dispense justice, He must pronounce all the world guilty, for that is the true fact. How then could God, who is a God of love and compassion, a God of mercy and grace, save any man? How could God receive a sinner into His presence when such are the facts? God must acquit or justify the righteous, and God must condemn the guilty.

We as parents are apt to find excuses for the misbehavior of our children. We do not sit as just judges on their conduct; when they disobey us we are prone to find some excuse for their conduct, for we do not want to administer justice as we know that it should be administered. So we explain away their conduct. In so doing, we are not dealing justly; we are not dealing on the basis of the facts in the case. Because they are our children, and we love them, we excuse and do not condemn the guilty. If it is the neighbor's children, we judge justly, but love keeps us from so judging our own.

God cannot deal so unjustly with men. God, in keeping with His holiness and righteousness and justice, must judge and condemn the guilty. But since all the world is guilty, how can any man be saved? That is the problem which God faced. How could He be just, and at the same time justify the one who does no more than believe? And this problem brings before us that which is the simplest and yet one of the most profound truths in all the Word of God: the doctrine of justification. It is to that doctrine that we would direct your attention as we discover from the Word how a just and loving God solved the problem so that He could receive sinners into His presence.

If you were to turn to Romans 8 you would find that the doctrine of justification is *logically* the conclusion of a process. I emphasize the word *logically,* for chronologically all God's saving work takes place instantaneously upon faith in the Lord Jesus Christ. There is no chronological development in the saving work of God. But there may be a logical development, and it is that logical progression that the Apostle refers to in Romans 8:29-30 when he says, ". . . whom he did foreknow, he also did predestinate to be conformed to the image of his Son, that he might be the firstborn among many brethren. Moreover whom he did predestinate, them he also called: and whom he called, them he also justified: and whom he justified, them he also glorified." You will notice the progression in Paul's presentation: it began with foreknowledge, moves on to predestination, then to a divine call, and then to justification. And justification is viewed as the climactic act of God in His saving work. It can be followed only by our glorification when we are transformed into the image of His Son in glory.

One becomes a child of God by the new birth. When one accepts Jesus Christ as a personal Savior, that one is placed in Christ Jesus by the baptizing work of the Holy Spirit. When one is placed in Christ Jesus he partakes of all that Christ is, just as when a bride is joined to her bridegroom she partakes of all that belongs to the husband.

In order to understand God's work of justification it is necessary to remember something that takes place when we are placed in Christ Jesus. First of all, according to II Corinthians 5:17, ". . . if any man be in Christ, he is a new creature: old things are passed away; behold, all things are become new." If any man be *in Christ*, old things have passed away. By that the Apostle is affirming the truth that all of our old relationships have been severed. We were born into this world related to Satan; he was the god of this world, the prince of the powers of the air, and we were members of his kingdom. We were related to the kingdom of darkness, to the kingdom of sin. We were related to Adam, for Adam was our head. We were related to sin, for sin not only characterized us but we were bondservants to sin. We were dominated by an old nature which was the commanding general who motivated and controlled us. Those are the old things that have been broken, or have "passed away." When we were placed in Christ Jesus we were made a new creation. We were related to a new Head, Jesus Christ. We were given a new divine nature; we were brought into a new Kingdom and made citizens of a new commonwealth. Our old relationships have been terminated and a new relationship has been instituted.

Some years ago, when we moved from Pennsylvania to Dallas, Texas to take up the work here in the Seminary, we left an old relationship and an old citizenship. We had been citizens of Pennsylvania. We paid our taxes there and by that recognized the existence of that citizenship. It was there that we had our residence. Our life was governed and controlled by the laws of Pennsylvania. When we moved to Texas and established legal residence here, we automatically severed the old relationship. By instituting a new relationship as citizens of Texas we automatically cut off the old citizenship. The Commonwealth of Pennsylvania could no longer levy taxes upon us; we were no longer subject to the laws of Pennsylvania as long as we were residing in Texas. The fact of the establishment of a new relationship automatically terminated the old relationship. The Apostle has established the fact that when we were put in Christ Jesus the old relationship was terminated and a new relationship was instituted because we were made a new creation in Christ.

The second thing the Apostle affirms is the fact that we, because we were in Christ Jesus, were *made righteous*. May I refer you to several passages of Scripture where this is plainly presented to us. In I Corinthians 1:30 Paul writes, "But of him are ye in Christ Jesus, who of God is made unto us wisdom, and righteousness, and sanctification, and redemption." To be in Christ Jesus is to be made righteous. Or again, in II Corinthians 5:21 Paul affirms the fact that Christ was made sin for us, He who knew no sin, that we might be made the *righteousness of God* in Him. Or again, in writing to the Philippians (3:7-9), the Apostle says, ". . . what things were gain to me, those I counted loss for Christ. Yea doubtless, and I count all things but loss for the excellency of the knowledge of Christ Jesus my Lord: for whom I have suffered the loss of all things, and do count them but dung, that I may win Christ, And be found in him, not having mine own righteousness, which is of the law, but that which is through the faith of Christ, the righteousness which is of God by faith." In these passages and in many others to which we could refer you, the Apostle is making very clear that the one who is placed in Christ Jesus is made righteous in the sight of God. God looks upon the one who is in Christ as clothed upon with the very righteousness of Jesus Christ so that there is no fault, no guilt, no basis for condemnation; we have been made righteous in Christ.

This means that the child of God who is in Christ Jesus has received forgiveness and has experienced redemption. May I point you to several Scriptures that bring this glorious fact to us. In Romans 3:24-25 Paul says, "Being justified freely by his grace through the redemption that is in Christ Jesus: Whom God hath set forth to be a propitiation through faith in his blood, to declare his righteousness for the remission of sins that are past, through the forbearance of God." May I emphasize several phrases in these verses. First of all, there is redemption in Christ Jesus. In a previous study we emphasized the fact that the New Testament doctrine of redemption teaches us that when we were bondslaves to sin, we were purchased in the slave market to be taken out of bondage to sin, to be set free in the glorious liberty that belongs to the children of God. We have been set free from sin's slavery, from sin's dominion, from sin's guilt, and sin's penalty. But further, Paul says that God has made Christ a propitiation through faith in His blood. There is a covering over for our sins so that God can look upon the world through the blood of Christ and can redeem men who were under the curse of God because there is propitiation through His blood. But further, in verse 25, Paul says that there is a remission of sins that are past, a putting away, a canceling out of the catalog of sins that was charged against the sinner. Before one could be accepted by God the sin question had to be settled, and when the Apostle says that we were made righteous it presupposes that God has dealt with our sins and has granted forgiveness, that God has finished redemption, that God has accomplished the work of remission of sins so that the truth affirmed in Ephesians 1:7 may be proclaimed. There Paul says, "In whom we have redemption through his blood, the forgiveness of sins, according to the riches of his grace." In this passage Paul reiterates what we saw in Romans 3: God has given redemption; God has granted forgiveness to the one who is in Christ Jesus so that our indebtedness has been removed, for the debt has been paid. We are new creatures in Christ; we are made righteous in Christ.

Then, in the third place, we discover in the Epistle to the Hebrews that we have been *perfected in Christ*. There the Apostle writes (10:14): "For by one offering he [God] hath perfected for ever them that are sanctified." The word "perfected" means "to be brought to full maturity." And when God looks at us in our position in Jesus Christ, He does not see us in our weakness, ignorance, and immaturity; He does not see us as stumbling, faltering babes in Christ—He sees us with all of the perfection that belongs to Jesus Christ. Thus God can view us as mature and adult sons in His own family.

In the fourth place, we discover from the Word of God that the one who is in Christ Jesus has *received the fullness of Christ*. We must remind ourselves of the truth given to us in John 1:16: "And of his fulness have all we received, and grace for grace." We believers have received His fullness! Then, writing to the Colossians, the Apostle Paul expands this truth as he explains the fullness that belonged to the Son: ". . . it pleased the Father that in him [that is, in the Son] should all fulness dwell" (1:19). All of the fullness, all of the completeness of God the Father resided in God the Son because the Son was one with the Father. Then, again in Colossians, Paul reaffirms the fact: "For in him [that is, in the Son] dwelleth all the fulness of the Godhead bodily" (2:9); or, to paraphrase the verse, "In Christ all the fulness of the Godhead made its dwelling in His body and ye are fulness or completeness in Him." The word translated "fulness" in Colossians 2:9 is the same word translated "complete" in Colossians 2:10. The glorious truth that Paul is affirming is that as in Christ dwelt all the fullness of the Godhead, so, since we are in Christ, all of the fullness of the Godhead dwells in us. That is only an expansion of what John affirms in John 1:16, ". . . of his fulness have all we received. . . ."

You see, from these four facts that we have presented, that when we are put in Christ Jesus by the work of the Holy Spirit we are brought into such union with the Son of God that all that belongs to the Son belongs to us. There is nothing that belongs to Him that He has not shared with us, apart from His essential deity. When then the Father looks upon us as the sons of God He sees us as He sees the Son of God.

All of these facts logically precede God's work of justification, for God first removes all sin, cancels out the indebtedness, then places us in Christ Jesus as a new creation, with all of the new relationships involved in that new creation. God gives to us the righteousness of Christ as our possession. God brings us to completion in the Son. God gives to us all of the fullness of the Godhead that dwelt in the Son as our portion. Then God can bring us before the tribunal of divine justice in order that He might examine us so as to proclaim justice in accordance with the facts. On the basis of these facts, only one verdict is possible—acquittal. Justification, then, is the divine pronouncement that the one who is in Christ Jesus is fully acceptable to Himself.

I would to God in your mind's eye you could see yourself being presented before the court over which God as a just Judge presides. In the outer room of that court, you as one who has received Christ as Saviour are being prepared to come into that court of justice. You are placed in Christ; you are made a new creation; you are robed with the righteousness of Christ; you are made mature in the Son. All the fullness of the Son has become your possession because you are in Christ. And then you march through that courtroom to take your place before the bar of justice upon whose bench a holy and a righteous God presides. God must pronounce a sentence in keeping with the facts in the case; God must justify the righteous and God must condemn the guilty. If you were to stand before that holy, righteous God outside of Christ and apart from the work of Christ, there is only one pronouncement which God could make: "Guilty, condemned, under wrath!" But when you stand in Christ Jesus before God's holy judgment, there is only one pronouncement which a righteous and just God can make: "Acquitted!" There is no basis for condemnation in you. On the authority of the Word of God, I say to you that if you are in Christ Jesus, there is no basis whatsoever upon which a just and holy God can pronounce any sentence other than "acquitted."

Justification does not depend upon altering the holiness of God, nor does it depend upon altering the fact that once you were a sinner. The judgment of God stands sure that all have sinned and come short of the glory of God. But God has so perfectly dealt with your sin, God has so met every demand upon the sinner, that when the believer is in Christ Jesus there is no more basis to exclude him than there is to exclude the eternal, holy Son of God Himself. God can acquit a man who once had been a sinner, but I submit to you on the authority of the Word of God, that God can justify *only* the one who is in Christ Jesus.

The Word of God devotes a good deal of teaching to this doctrine of justification. To present a good many facets of this truth briefly, I would like to mention seven passages which give to us seven facets of the doctrine of justification. First of all, we learn that a man is justified *by God*. In Romans 8:30 we read, ". . . whom he [God] called, them he also justified. . . ." Or again, in verse 33: "Who shall lay any thing to the charge of God's elect? It is God that justifieth." In this passage we see the first great fact that *the source* of justification is in the holy, righteous God. In Romans 3:26 the Apostle likewise said, ". . . that he [that is, God] might be just, and the justifier of him which believeth in Jesus." This truth recognizes the fact that all sin is basically sin against God. While sin may injure the individual, or injure another man, or injure society, inherently all sin is against God. A man may discharge his responsibility to another man, or to the state, but that does not mean that he has discharged his responsibility to God. That responsibility is not satisfied until God, a just Judge, has been satisfied. First of all, then, we must be justified by God.

But, in the second place, we are justified *by blood*. And in a passage such as Romans 3:24-26 we have revealed *the ground* of justification. God planned for our righteousness. God also provided righteousness and that righteousness is solely through the shed blood of Jesus Christ. We have redemption through His blood (v. 24) ; we have propitiation through His blood; we have remission of sins—all through His blood. Blood is the ground of justification because the Scripture reveals that life is in the blood. And when Jesus Christ shed His blood, Jesus Christ laid down His life. It was His life in place of your life, His death in place of your death, so that you might receive remission of sin through His blood.

In the third place we discover that we are justified *by faith*. Faith is *the instrument* of justification. See it again in Romans 3:28: ". . . we conclude that a man is justified by faith without the deeds of the law"; in Romans 4:5: ". . . to him that worketh not, but believeth on him that justifieth the ungodly, his faith is counted for righteousness"; or in Romans 5:1: "Therefore being justified by faith, we have peace with God through our Lord Jesus Christ." Here we discover the fact that it is not works which bring justification. No man can pay God for the indebtedness which he has incurred; no man can come before the bar of divine justice and offer to work out his payment if given enough time, for eternity would not be long enough to discharge our responsibility to God. A man is justified not by works, but by faith. That is why we continually invite men to receive Jesus Christ by faith as a personal Saviour, for apart from faith it is impossible to please God.

In the fourth place we discover in this passage in Romans that we are justified *by grace,* and this gives to us the very *essence of justification.* Paul writes, in Romans 3:24, "Being justified freely by his grace. . . ." Grace is God's unmerited favor bestowed upon sinners by which God sets aside what they deserve in order to confer upon them that which they never could deserve. Paul adds here that we are justified freely. The word translated "freely" is the word which means "without a cause," without any cause within us. God did not justify us because He saw some attractiveness in us, or because God saw some inherent goodness in us, or because we were worth saving; we were justified without any cause in us whatsoever. God has justified us by His own infinite, matchless grace.

In the fifth place, when we turn to I Corinthians 6:11 we discover that we were justified by *the Spirit.* After giving to us the list of the sins of the flesh in verses 9 and 10, Paul says, "And such were some of you: but ye are washed, but ye are sanctified, but ye are justified in the name of the Lord Jesus, and by the Spirit of our God." The Spirit who is *the agent* in the new birth puts us in Christ Jesus. And because we have been placed in Christ Jesus, God, a righteous Judge, can pronounce a sentence of acquittal, not because we had never sinned but because we are in Christ. It is the work of the Spirit that renders it possible for us to hear that verdict, "acquitted before this bar of justice."

In the sixth place, from James 2 we discover that we are justified *by works.* Here we have *the evidence of justification.* James says, "Was not Abraham our father justified by works . . . ?"(v. 21). "Ye see then how that by works a man is justified . . ." (v. 24). "Likewise also was not Rahab the harlot justified by works . . . ?" (v. 25). These have reference to justification before men. After a man has been declared acquitted by God, he will evidence his acquittal before men by the righteousness which his position in Christ produces. A man is not justified before God by his works, but man evidences his justification before men by his works.

Finally we find that we are justified *in Christ.* This gives us the *position* of the justified one. Read it again in II Corinthians 5:21: God "hath made him to be sin for us, who knew no sin; that we might be made the righteousness of God in him [Christ]." It is because we are in Him that justification is possible. Justified by God, righteousness planned; justified by blood, righteousness provided; justified by faith, righteousness procured; justified by grace, the divine principle by which righteousness operates; justified by the Spirit, the power by which we are made righteous; justified by works, righteousness proved; justified in Christ, righteousness possessed. God called Abraham apart to Himself. God said, "Abraham, even in your old age you are going to have a son. Look at the stars of heaven and number them if you can. Your seed will be as multitudinous as the stars in heaven." And Abraham heard the promise of God and Abraham believed God. Abraham, in his heart, said "Amen" to the promise of God and God testified that Abraham was declared righteous, or justified, because he believed God.

God's sentence has been passed upon all men. *All* have sinned and come short of the glory of God. How then can God receive that one who is under condemnation into His presence? God, in infinite wisdom, and by the work of the Holy Spirit, puts that sinner in Christ Jesus, makes him a new creation, makes him righteous in Christ, gives to him mature standing in Christ, imparts all the fullness of Christ. Then, having done that, God the Father examines him and says, "There is no basis upon which I must condemn him, but there is adequate basis upon which I may receive him." And, as Paul writes in Ephesians 1:6, we are "accepted in the beloved." That is why the Apostle John can write and say, concerning Christ, ". . . as he is, so are we in this world" (I, 4:17). As Jesus Christ cannot be brought into judgment before God, because He is the holy, sinless Son of God, no more can the one be brought into condemnation who is in Christ Jesus, for when he stands before God, God says, "I accept him in the Beloved. I declare him to be acceptable to My righteousness and holiness. While I cannot acquit the guilty, this one is no longer guilty because he is in Christ Jesus. I declare that one who was under condemnation to be justified." That is your position before the Father if you have accepted Christ as your Saviour.

If you should be without Christ as your Saviour, on the authority of the Word of God I submit to you that when you stand in judgment before a righteous God, God as a just God can make only one pronouncement. Since He cannot clear the guilty, God must say, "Depart from Me, ye wicked, into everlasting fire prepared for the devil and his angels." If you accept Christ as your Saviour there is only one pronouncement God, in righteousness and justice, can make—"Accepted in the Beloved." Which sentence will be yours?

11 ◆ Sanctification

I Corinthians 1:1-3, 26-31

THERE ARE FEW doctrines so misunderstood as that which we consider now—the doctrine of sanctification. The average child of God instinctively recalls the fanaticism and excesses attached to the doctrine of sanctification, and instinctively withdraws from it, relegating this precious teaching of the Word of God to certain fringe groups. Consequently, we have withdrawn from giving rightful place to the teaching concerning this important truth.

There are certain basic errors which we would do well to call to your attention at the outset so that our minds might be relieved of them. Sanctification, in its primary usage in the Scripture, does not refer to improvement in practical holiness. If this were the meaning, it would be impossible for God to sanctify Himself, for God does not improve in holiness. Yet Scripture reveals that both God the Father and God the Son sanctify themselves. We thus must conclude that it is an error to affirm that sanctification deals, primarily, with improvement in holiness.

A second error that must be set aside is that sanctification implies a state of holiness in which it is impossible for the child of God to sin. Sanctification itself does not imply a state of holiness; this is witnessed by Paul's Letter to the Corinthians, a church beset by every form of doctrinal and practical and moral error and yet a church spoken of by the Apostle Paul as having been sanctified. If sanctification referred to a state of holiness, then it could never be said that the Corinthians were saints and had been sanctified.

When we examine the Word of God, we find three words in our English text that are pertinent to our study of this important doctrine: "sanctify," "holy," and "saint." It seems as though all three of these words have been misinterpreted and misunderstood, and much of the error concerning this doctrine—and much of the fanaticism in practice arising out of this doctrine—has arisen through a failure to understand these three words. The word "sanctify" occurs more than one hundred times in the Old Testament, and more than thirty times in the New Testament. The word, in its basic usage, means "to set apart." It does not mean "to make holy"; it does not mean "to be holy" or "to progress in holiness."

I would direct you to John 17:18-19 where in our Lord's prayer to the Father He says, "As thou hast sent me into the world, even so have I also sent them into the world. And for their sakes I sanctify myself, that they also might be sanctified through the truth." Our Lord was referring to the fact that He was set apart by the Father to do a work. He was sanctified, or set apart, to go into the world; and because He had been set apart, in perfect obedience He fulfilled the will of the Father. Jesus Christ was about to depart to be with the Father, and it was His desire to set apart others who would reveal the Father to the world as He had revealed the Father to the world. The disciples were set apart by Christ to go as His representatives, as His ambassadors, to reveal the Son, so that the Son might continue to reveal the Father. Now, this "setting apart" Christ called "sanctification" when He said, ". . . and for their sakes I sanctify myself [or, I set myself apart]. . . ." He set Himself apart to the cross; He set Himself apart to physical death; He set Himself apart to separation from the Father; He set Himself apart totally and completely to the will of God so that He could say, "I come to do thy will, O God" (Hebrews 10:9). This passage reveals what the word "sanctify" basically means: "to set apart."

The second word, "holy," is used over 400 times in the Old Testament, and some twelve times in the New Testament. The word "holy" means "to be set apart from what is unholy." The root word is related to the word "sanctification." In Hebrews 7:26 this statement is made concerning Christ: "For such an high priest became us, who is holy, harmless, undefiled, separate from sinners, and made higher than the heavens." Jesus Christ, our High Priest, is holy! Now, what did it mean for Jesus Christ to be holy? Notice the words that follow, which explain the holiness of Jesus Christ: He was harmless, He was undefiled, He was separate from sinners. Underline the word *separate,* or *separated from sinners.* The Lord Jesus Christ was guilty of no sin; He did no sin, and yet He was made sin for us, that we might be made the righteousness of God in Him. Jesus Christ is said to be holy because He is set apart, or set off, or divided from that which is unholy. We would conclude, then, that the word "holy" has the same basic connotation as the word "sanctify"—that is, "set apart."

The third word is "saint," which is used sixty-two times in the New Testament in reference to believers. It is the commonest word used in the New Testament to refer to a child of God. The children of God are called "saints." We observe this fact in I Corinthians 1:2: "Unto the church of God which is at Corinth, to them that are sanctified [or, set apart] in Christ Jesus, called [to be] saints. . . ." You will notice that your English text reads, ". . . called *to be* saints . . . ," and many have misunderstood this because they have concluded that we were called in order that eventually we might become saints. That is not what the Apostle is writing, for he is writing to all those who are in Christ Jesus. He says that they have been sanctified—that is, set apart unto God in Christ Jesus—and because they have been set apart, they are called "saints" by God. The word "saint" in the original text comes from the same Greek root as the word "holy." The word "saint" means simply "one who has been set apart unto God."

We observe then that the three words have a common connotation, and they all signify *that which has been set apart,* or the one who has been set apart unto God. We observe further that the words "sanctify," "holy" and "saint" primarily have to do with one's position, not with one's experience or one's practice. This has to do with the divine viewpoint. When God looks at His child, He sees His child as set apart unto Himself; He sees His child having been set apart from sin; He sees His child as one who is a saint, beloved of the Father. This then is our position.

We want to present now three aspects of the believer's sanctification, three aspects of the believer's holiness, three aspects of the believer's sainthood. First of all, Scripture teaches what we refer to as *positional sanctification.* In I Corinthians 6:9-10 we read, "Know ye not that the unrighteous shall not inherit the kingdom of God? Be not deceived: neither fornicators, nor idolators, nor adulterers, nor effeminate, nor abusers of themselves with mankind, Nor thieves, nor covetous, nor drunkards, nor revilers, nor extortioners, shall inherit the kingdom of God." The Apostle, in that heinous catalogue of sins, revealed the life that characterized the citizens of the city of Corinth. Given over to a licentious religious system, they practiced all manner of excesses. But the Apostle wanted to show that those who once practiced Corinthianism had been separated unto God from that kind of life. And Paul proceeds, in verse 11: "And such were some of you: but ye are washed, but ye are sanctified, but ye are justified in the name of the Lord Jesus, and by the Spirit of our God." The Apostle was revealing the position which the Corinthian believers held in the sight of God. They had been sanctified, that is, set apart unto God. They had been made holy, that is, separated from the practices that once characterized them. They had become saints, holy ones in the family of God. This was not yet their experience, for as you read through the Corinthian Epistle, you will see that they lacked practical holiness, and they lacked practical godliness and righteousness. The church was marked by strife, discord, and division; it was marked by immorality; it was marked by doctrinal heresies. All of these the Apostle had to correct, and yet, in the sight of God, they had been sanctified and justified.

When these Corinthians were said to be sanctified, the Apostle was emphasizing that which logically is the result of the saving grace of God. They had been redeemed by the blood of Christ; they had been cleansed by the blood of Christ; they had been forgiven all sins; they had been made righteous through Christ; they had been justified through God's legal declaration that they were acceptable to God; they had been set apart unto God. This sanctification was the result of the whole saving work of God that gave to them the righteousness of Christ and set those apart unto God as God's possession. This is affirmed in I Corinthians 1:2 when Paul says, "Unto the church of God which is at Corinth, to them that are sanctified in Christ Jesus. . . ." Here is a completed work, a work that needs no repetition, for they have been set apart as God's possession. God has put His name upon them, has imputed the righteousness of Christ to them; they stand as recipients of God's grace, and they can be said to have been sanctified.

In the Epistle to the Hebrews we have this same truth reaffirmed, for the Apostle says, "By the which will we are sanctified through the offering of the body of Jesus Christ once for all" (10:10). The phrase "once for all" grammatically may refer back to the offering of the body of Christ, which was done once for all, or it may refer back to the word "sanctify"—"by the which will we are sanctified once and for all." And the Apostle was affirming the truth that, when God called us and redeemed us and made us righteous in Christ and justified us through the blood of Christ, God set us apart to Himself, and this work was done with a finality. Positionally, it need never be repeated and can never be repeated, for we are His own. Then again, in verse 14 of the same chapter, the Apostle says, "For by one offering [that is, the offering up of Jesus Christ] he hath perfected for ever them that are sanctified." Those that have been set aside are mature, adult sons in the family of the Father. I submit to you, child of God, that this is one of the most precious truths that you can get hold of. In the sight of God you have been set apart as His possession. You belong to Him by right of purchase. You have been declared acceptable by His legal act of justifying you through Christ. You have been set apart unto God. This is true of the weakest and the youngest believer in the Lord Jesus Christ. This does not depend upon your maturity, upon your knowledge, upon your practice of godliness, or your own righteousness. This is a divine work in which God sets us apart to Himself.

The writer to the Ephesians emphasizes this truth: "Husbands, love your wives, even as Christ also loved the church, and gave himself for it; That He might sanctify and cleanse it with the washing of water by the word" (5:25-26). We were redeemed! We were cleansed! We were washed, so that we might be set apart unto God. It is as though a shepherd were to go into a fold to separate his sheep, and, as the sheep file out the door, he would have said to a fellow shepherd, "This one is yours, this one is mine, this one is yours, this one is mine," and so on, until each sheep had passed out of that fold. There were certain sheep that were set apart unto the shepherd. They were sanctified to the shepherd. And child of God, you have been set apart for God. God has placed His name and His identifying seal, the Holy Spirit, upon you. Such is your position in Jesus Christ.

In Ephesians 4:24 the Apostle says, ". . . that ye might put on the new man, which after God is created in righteousness and true holiness." We are new creatures in Christ Jesus because we are a new creation. We have been made righteous, and we have been given "true holiness." Such is our possession; such is our position in the Lord Jesus Christ.

We come to the second aspect: the experiential side of sanctification. The child of God who has been sanctified, or set apart unto God, is exhorted to let his experience conform to his position; and the problem in the Christian life is to bring experience up to position. The Apostle has a good deal to say about the child of God setting himself apart, experientially, unto God. We are familiar with Romans 12:1: "I beseech you therefore, brethren, by the mercies of God, that ye present your bodies a living sacrifice. . . ." The child of God who presents his body a living sacrifice is sanctifying or setting himself apart unto God. We find this same truth in Romans 6:13 where the Apostle writes, "Neither yield ye [or present ye] your members as instruments of unrighteousness unto sin: but yield yourselves [or present your members] unto God, as those that are alive from the dead, and your members as instruments of righteousness unto God." The verb "yield" in this verse is the same verb used in Romans 12:1 and translated "present." It means "to set oneself apart unto God." This is practical or experiential sanctification. The Christian life depends upon the believer setting himself apart by an act of his will so that he is controlled by the Spirit of God; no longer to live under the control of sin, nor to live under the control of law, nor to live under the control of the flesh, but to live under the control of the Spirit of God. Experiential sanctification, then, begins with the act of presenting oneself unto the Lord Jesus Christ, and presenting oneself to control by the Spirit of God.

The result of this presentation to the Holy Spirit's empowerment is freedom from sin in daily life. Read again several verses from Romans 6. Verses 14-16 read, ". . . sin shall not have dominion over you: for ye are not under the law, but under grace. What then? shall we sin, because we are not under the law, but under grace? God forbid. Know ye not, that to whom ye yield [or present] yourselves servants to obey, his servants ye are to whom ye obey; whether of sin unto death, or of obedience unto righteousness?" The Apostle emphasizes the truth that the child of God who presents himself as a living sacrifice to Jesus Christ, to be controlled by the Spirit of God, will not live in sin. The Apostle John, writing in I John 2:1, says, ". . .

these things write I unto you, that ye sin not." God's purpose for His child is that he should live in Jesus Christ. God desires to reproduce Himself in His children so that He might be glorified through His children. And when we present ourselves, or sanctify ourselves, or yield ourselves to the Spirit's control, the Spirit will reproduce in us His own fruit, that we might live to the glory of God.

This practical holiness will manifest itself, as Peter tells us in II Peter 3:18, in our growth in grace and knowledge. Peter says: ". . . grow in grace, and in the knowledge of our Lord and Saviour Jesus Christ." We often refer to this as progressive sanctification—where Christ, who was formed in us by the Holy Spirit when we were born into God's family, is being reproduced in us, more and more, by the Spirit's control. In II Corinthians 3-18 Paul says, ". . . we all, with open face beholding as in a glass the glory of the Lord, are changed [or, literally, are being changed] into the same image from glory to glory, even as by the Spirit of the Lord." Paul emphasizes in that passage that there is a work of the Holy Spirit by which we are progressively being conformed in our daily experience to the Lord Jesus Christ. We are being changed into the same image, going from glory to glory. Our position before God is that we are sanctified, set apart unto God; our experience is that we are being sanctified in daily life, by the Spirit's power, as we grow in grace and in knowledge, and as we are controlled by the Spirit of God.

The child of God recognizes that no day is lived in practical righteousness and holiness. We stumble and fall, in thought, word, and deed. There is sin of omission, and sin of commission, and we stand convicted before a holy and righteous God. The Apostle John has given us a solution to this problem in I John 1:9: "If we confess our sins, he is faithful and just to forgive us our sins, and to cleanse us from all unrighteousness." Jesus Christ can be reproduced in the life of the child of God because the Spirit of God can convict the child of God of his unholiness and can bring him to the place of confession so that sin might be forgiven and the believer might be restored, and that the Spirit might continue His work of reproducing Jesus Christ in the life of the child of God.

But is there no termination to this struggle? Must we always be subject to Satan's snare? We recognize that as long as we are in the flesh, we are living in an unredeemed body. We are living with an unredeemed sin-nature within us which may manifest its fruit unless we live by the Spirit's power. But the Word of God reveals a third precious truth concerning sanctification, and that is our *ultimate sanctification*. The Apostle John so clearly presents this truth in I John 3:2: "Beloved, now are we the sons of God, and it doth not yet appear what we shall be: but we know that, when he shall appear, we shall be like him; for we shall see him as he is." Observe carefully what John wrote. We will be like Christ in that we will be sinless, we will be deathless, and we will be brought to maturity in spiritual things. We will be like Him. But when? When we are old, and gray-haired? *No!* When He shall appear. It is the coming of Jesus Christ to gather His own to Himself that will bring us, God's saints, to a realization of the position which is ours. At the coming of Christ—when the body of Christ has been completed, when the last redeemed one has been brought into God's family—we will be translated out of this sphere of sin and into His glory, and we shall be like Him. Then our experience will conform to our position throughout the unending ages of eternity.

Jude, in his benediction (v. 25), gives us this same precious expectation, for he extols Christ who "is able to keep you from falling, and to present you faultless before the presence of his glory with exceeding joy." Jude was anticipating our ultimate sanctification when our experience will conform to our position through the transforming work of the coming Son of God. The Apostle Paul, in Ephesians 5, speaks concerning our positional sanctification and our ultimate sanctification. Paul gives us the work of Christ in verse 26: "That he might sanctify and cleanse it with the washing of water by the word." And what is the ultimate purpose? "That he might present it to himself a glorious church, not having spot, or wrinkle, or any such thing; but that it should be holy [sanctified, set apart] and without blemish" (v. 27). This is our position, praise God, in the sight of God. But we have to confess that this is not our practice; for we, as a people, as a church, and as individuals, could not say of ourselves that we do not have spot or wrinkle or any such thing, or that we are holy and without blemish in our daily practice. But the Apostle is anticipating that glorious time which will come when God's purpose to sanctify unto Himself a set-apart people will be realized. When He transforms us into His presence, into the likeness of Christ, we shall attain that for which we were called.

On what does this full-orbed sanctification rest? How can we be sanctified? May I mention to you that sanctification is the work of the triune God. In I Thessalonians 5:23, God the Father is the One who sanctifies us. In Ephesians 5:26 it is the Son who sanctifies us. In Romans 15:16, Paul says the Holy Spirit is the One who sanctifies. God the Father, God the Son, God the Holy Spirit—all are active agents in our redemption. God the Father planned, chose, and called; God the Son gave His life for our redemption; God the Holy Spirit applies the benefits of Christ's redemption to those who are sanctified in Christ Jesus. As our redemption is the work of the triune God, so no less is our sanctification the work of the triune God. God has set us apart to Himself; the Son has cleansed those who have been set apart to God; the Holy Spirit is setting apart in daily practice those who have been sanctified in Christ.

We would like to mention, just briefly, certain facts. First of all, we were sanctified *in Christ Jesus;* I Corinthians 1:2—". . . to them that are sanctified in Christ Jesus . . ."; and in I Corinthians 1:30— "But of him are ye in Christ Jesus, who of God is made unto us wisdom, and righteousness, and sanctification. . . ." The phrase "in Christ Jesus" gives us the *sphere* of our sanctification. We are set apart because we are in Christ Jesus.

In the second place, we are sanctified *by the Word of God.* The Word of God is *the channel* through which this sanctification comes to us. Our Lord said (John 17:17): "Sanctify them through thy truth; thy word is truth." And in Ephesians 5:26, Paul says, "That he might sanctify and cleanse it with the washing of water by the word." The Word of God is an active agent in setting us apart unto God, for the Word reveals the purpose of the Father, the plan of the Father, the provision of the Father, the ultimate destiny of those who have been set apart in Christ Jesus.

From Hebrews 13:12 we learn that we are sanctified *by blood.* The Apostle writes, "Wherefore Jesus also, that he might sanctify the people with his own blood, suffered without the gate." Sanctification has *its basis* in the blood of Christ because the blood of Christ is that which cleanses the sinner. It is only as the sinner is cleansed that he can be set apart from his sin unto God. So blood is the basis upon which our sanctification rests.

The Apostle also writes in Hebrews 10:10: ". . . we are sanctified through the offering of the body of Jesus Christ once for all." He is focusing our attention here upon *the cross* of Christ. The cross of Christ was *the place* where our sanctification was made possible through the death of Christ. Writing in Galatians 6:14, the Apostle shows how the cross has sanctified him, or set him apart from the world, and set him apart unto God, for he says, "God forbid that I should glory, save in the cross of our Lord Jesus Christ, by whom the world is crucified unto me, and I unto the world." There was a separation, or a sanctification, that took place on the cross; and the cross is God's barrier between you and what you were as a sinner, between you and what you were as a citizen in the world. The cross of Christ prevents you from ever going back into that from which you have been set apart by God. We were set apart by God by the death of Christ on the cross.

Finally, according to Acts 26:18, we were sanctified by *faith*. Here we have *the means* by which this sanctification is appropriated, for Paul testifies of himself that God had sent him "To open their eyes, and to turn them from darkness to light, and from the power of Satan unto God, that they may receive forgiveness of sins, and inheritance among them which are sanctified by faith that is in me." Faith is that which relates one to Jesus Christ, so that in Christ Jesus the believer might be set apart unto God.

Child of God, I would that the truth of your sanctification could be burned indelibly upon your consciousness, that you should realize that you *have been* set apart unto God. This is your present position. In this you may glory and revel, for you have been sanctified. You are called by God, a saint. You have been made holy and righteous. Would to God that you could realize that one who has been set apart unto God is expected to live a new kind of life to the glory of God. May God the Holy Spirit conform your daily practice to your present position as a sanctified one, so that you might live a sanctified life, or a life set apart unto God. May God give you the hope of your ultimate conformity to Christ, when your experience shall conform to your position, and you shall be like Him, for you shall see Him as He is. Only a holy and righteous God could work so marvelously on behalf of sinners to bring them to sanctification in Christ Jesus.

12 • Security

SOME TIME AGO, an agitated young lady who was attending our church came to me and asked if I would talk with her following the service. My wife and I, together with a couple who were much interested in her salvation, went to her home. When we sat down, she looked at me and said, "You preachers make me sick! You stand up there with a smug complacency, telling people that they can know they are saved, when I would give my right arm to know I am saved." She continued, "If you are not a hypocrite, and you mean what you said—that people can know they are saved—tell me how they can know." To cover up her nervousness, she fumbled for a pack of cigarettes and lit one after another, as through a haze of smoke I tried to make the gospel plain to her, and tell her how one could be safe and secure in Jesus Christ. At five minutes to midnight, she gave her heart to the Lord Jesus Christ and accepted Him as her Saviour. I can still remember the change in her countenance as she said, "I will have to take back what I said about your being smug and complacent when you talked about knowing you were saved." Then she said, "Now I know, too."

The question that she faced (and for which she long had sought an answer) is a question that many would like to have settled for themselves. They would like to feel secure; they would like to know that the question of eternal destiny has been settled. They would like to know that sins have been forgiven. They would like to know that they have peace with God.

As we consider with you the doctrine of security, we recognize immediately that our security is related to the kind of salvation which God has provided for sinners. Has God provided salvation, or has God provided a chance for salvation to those who accept Jesus Christ as a personal Saviour? Related to this is the question, Who is responsible for man's salvation? Does God do a saving work for men? Or do men contribute something to their own salvation? For it stands self-evident that, if God does the work, God will make no mistake and there will be no failure. If man contributes something to his own salvation, man may make mistakes and man may lose his salvation because he did not fulfill his obligation.

We recognize that this is a controversial subject, and it has divided theologians into different schools of thought. But we want to examine the Word of God to see what Scripture teaches concerning the kind of salvation God provides, and the promise God makes to men who receive Christ as a personal Saviour. It will not be possible for us to go extensively into this great doctrine; we will treat it only in outline form. But I trust that we shall say enough to whet your appetite, to get you to delve into the Scriptures yourself, so that you may rest in the security that belongs to the child of God.

Those who teach that a man can lose his salvation, or fall from grace, as they often refer to it, are not without Scriptures which seem to support their position. There are a number of different groups of Scriptures which are used—and, I believe, misused—to support the doctrine that a man can be saved today but lose his salvation tomorrow and may need to be saved all over again. This would be a complete study in itself, and I can only make a few suggestions along this line. First, there are those passages which are related to the nation Israel, in which the nation is warned that it will be set aside by God if it continues in disobedience. For instance, in the Gospel of Matthew 18 there is the parable of the king making a reckoning with his servant—and there are some unfaithful servants who are banished from the king's presence. This parable was designed to teach not that a man loses his salvation, but rather that a privileged servant-nation may be set aside if it persists in disobedience and unbelief, and rejection of Jesus Chrst. Many of the Old Testament passages used to support the doctrine that a man may lose his salvation fall into this classification.

Then there are passages that relate to the apostates in the last days. For instance, in I Timothy 4:1-3, Paul says, ". . . the Spirit speaketh expressly, that in the latter times some shall depart from the faith, giving heed to seducing spirits, and doctrines of devils; Speaking lies in hypocrisy; having their conscience seared with a hot iron; Forbidding to marry, and commanding to abstain from meats, which God hath created to be received with thanksgiving of them which believe and know the truth." These apostates were never redeemed men, never born again; they never possessed eternal life but they held to a form of godliness while denying the power thereof—and of such we are warned.

There is a third class of passages which relate to professors—those who professed to know Christ but never knew Him, in actuality. Perhaps John 15:6 would fall into this classification: "If a man abide not in me, he is cast forth as a branch, and is withered; and men gather them, and cast them into the fire, and they are burned." Christ is not teaching that a man who has been saved will be cast into hell; but such professors will be, because there is no truth behind their profession.

There are passages that contain warnings to God's children. The problem passage in Hebrews 6 seems to fall into this classification, for the Apostle warns that it is impossible for those who have received God's heavenly gift and tasted the powers of the age to come to renew them again to repentance if they should fall away. He is not threatening men with a loss of salvation, but is showing believers that they cannot erase the record of failure by going back and being saved all over again. Therefore, the record must stand. There are many warnings to God's children that would fall into this classification.

Then, in the fifth place, there are those passages which relate to the loss of rewards. Believers are continually warned that if they are unfaithful, they will lose their reward: for instance, in John 15:2: "Every branch in me that beareth not fruit he taketh away: and every branch that beareth fruit, he purgeth it, that it may bring forth more fruit"; or, in I Corinthians 3, Paul reminds believers that they shall be saved, yet so as by fire. A believer may lose his reward, but loss of reward is not synonymous with loss of his salvation.

There is the passage in Galatians 5:4, finally, that speaks of falling from grace. The Apostle Paul is not talking about losing one's salvation, but rather about abandoning the grace principle by which we were saved and by which we are to live. Saved Jews who tried to live by the Law would be leaving the grace principle.

Now the observation that we make as we look at these different categories of passages which have been used to deny security to the child of God, is that not one of these has to do with the question of salvation, or of the continuance of salvation, or of the duration of a man's salvation when he has been saved. The question of salvation is not in any one of these realms, and so it is applying Scripture wrongly to take these passages and suggest that they teach loss of salvation.

When we come to the positive side of the teaching of Scripture, we want to suggest that the believer's security, or safety, is related to the saving work of God. Briefly, we want to mention the work of the Father, and the work of the Son, and the work of the Holy Spirit on behalf of the sinner who comes to God by faith in Christ, to show that "more secure is no one ever, than the loved ones of the Saviour."

The *work of the Father,* first of all, is the basis for the believer's security. May we suggest, then, that *the purpose* of God is basic to our security. In Ephesians 1:4 the Apostle writes that God "hath chosen us in him before the foundation of the world, that we should be holy and without blame before him in love." God has chosen us, that we should be holy and without blame. Again in Hebrews 2:10, the Apostle writes that it was God's avowed purpose to bring many sons into glory. It is easy for you to see that if God purposes to make men holy and blameless, and purposes to bring His sons into glory, if one son is lost, then God's purpose has been defeated and God's purpose has not been realized. First of all, then, God's purpose to populate heaven with His children for eternity demands the security of the believer.

In the second place, the *power of God* to save and to keep the one who comes to Him through Christ is a sufficient basis for our security. Read the words of our Lord (John 10:29) as He asserts, "My Father, which gave them me, is greater than all; and no man is able to pluck them out of my Father's hand." The key to this verse is in the word "able." God is *able* to keep. The only reason that God would not be able to keep is that there is someone stronger than He who could snatch the believer from His hand. Since God is sovereign and supreme and omnipotent, there is no power that can rise against Him so that He would be unable to keep those who had come to Him through Jesus Christ. The Apostle emphasizes this same truth again in Romans 8:31-34: "If God be for us, who can be against us? He that spared not his own Son, but delivered him up for us all, how shall he not with him also freely give us all things? Who shall lay any thing to the charge of God's elect? It is God that justifieth. Who is he that condemneth? It is Christ that died, yea rather, that is risen, who is even at the right hand of God, who also maketh intercession for us." And then in verses 38-39 Paul adds, "For I am persuaded, that neither death, nor life, nor angels, nor principalities, nor powers, nor things present, nor things to come, Nor height, nor depth, nor any other creature, shall be able to separate us from the love of God, which is in Christ Jesus our Lord." The Apostle mentions every spiritual and natural enemy of a man, and shows us that there is no enemy with sufficient power to overthrow God's purpose and plan, and to take the believer out of God's charge. God is able to keep that which we have committed unto Him against that day.

Not only the purpose of God but also the *promise of God* is a basis for our security. We go into a familiar passage such as John 3:16 where it is made so clear: " . . . God so loved the world, that he gave his only begotten Son, that whosoever believeth in him should not perish, but have everlasting life." Notice the two aspects of the promise: negatively, he shall not perish; positively, he shall have everlasting life! Or again, in John 5:24, we read, "Verily, verily, I say unto you, He that heareth my word, and believeth on him that sent me, hath everlasting life, and shall not come into condemnation; but is passed from death unto life." We see in this verse the same twofold aspect: the negative, he shall not come into condemnation, or judgment; the positive side, he has already passed from death into life. When God offers a man life, God offers a man only one kind of life, and that is eternal life. Eternal life is the life of God, and as God's life could never be terminated by death, so the life of God, given to the child of God, could never be terminated. We submit to you that the promise of God to give eternal life to the one who accepts Christ as his Saviour is a sufficient basis for our security.

Finally, the *love of God* for those whom He has redeemed is a basis for our security. In Romans 5:7-9 we read, "For scarcely for a righteous man will one die: yet peradventure for a good man some would even dare to die. But God commendeth his love toward us, in that, while we were yet sinners, Christ died for us. Much more then, being now justified by his blood, we shall be saved from wrath through him." Why are we saved? Because God loved us; because Christ died for us; because we have been justified by His blood. And as though the love of God were not sufficient cause for our security, the Apostle adds the fact that Christ died and that we have been justified by His blood. Therefore, the plan of the Father, and the power of God to save and keep, and the promise of God of eternal life, and the love of God for those for whom Christ died— all are the basis for the security of the believer.

Not only was God the Father active in planning salvation, but Jesus Christ was active in providing salvation. The provision of the Son is a basis for our security. We note in Romans 5:8 the first great work, or provision, of the Son upon which our security rests, the *death of Christ*. Paul affirms the truth that "Christ died for us." Again, in Romans 8:1, Paul asserts, "There is therefore now no condemnation [judgment] to them which are in Christ Jesus. . . ." In I John 2:2 John writes that Christ "is the propitiation [the covering over] for our sins: and not for ours only, but also for the sins of the whole world." In writing to the Hebrews (5:8-9) the author states, "Though he were a Son, yet learned he obedience by the things which he suffered; And being made perfect [that is, in His suffering, or having completed His sufferings], he became the author of eternal salvation unto all them that obey him." He became the Author of *eternal* salvation because He suffered and died for sinful men. When Jesus Christ was on the cross, He could look up to the Father and shout triumphantly, "It is finished!" His death was a satisfaction for the sin of the world. His death was the payment to God for the indebtedness of the human race. His death made provision that all men might be saved, and the whole world was rendered savable because of the death of Jesus Christ. Jesus Christ, in His death, did not make a token payment or a down payment toward our sins, so that we are expected to pick up the balance and continue the monthly installments; Christ paid sin's price. Because this price has been paid, the individual who accepts Christ as personal Saviour is given a certificate of manumission: he is set free, discharged from his obligation and indebtedness to God. The record that was black has been made white and clean, and the sinner stands accepted in the Beloved, because Christ died for our sins.

In the second place, the *resurrection of Christ* is a provision by the Son for our security. In Ephesians 2:6, Paul says that God "hath raised us up together, and made us sit together in heavenly places in Christ Jesus." When Jesus Christ rose from the dead He included in His resurrection all those who are in Christ. God sees us as seated in the heavenlies, where no enemy could come to contest our right to be there in God's presence. Paul, in Romans 4:25, tells us that Jesus Christ "was delivered for our offences, and was raised again for our justification"; or better, ". . . because our justification was accomplished." The basis for the sinner's acceptance before God was provided by the death of Christ, and when provision had been made there was no reason why Jesus Christ should continue in the bonds of sin. So He rose victorious and triumphant because the basis for men's acceptance by God had been laid. When we have been resurrected with Christ, seated with Him in the heavenlies, no enemy can come to challenge our right to be at home in the presence of the Father. It was not only the death of Christ but also the resurrection of Christ that is the basis of our security.

In the third place, when Christ ascended into heaven He ascended to become an Advocate for God's children. His work as *Advocate* is a basis for our security. Writing to the Hebrews (9:24), the Apostle says, "For Christ is not entered into the holy places made with hands, which are the figures of the true; but into heaven itself, now to appear in the presence of God for us." Christ appears in the presence of God *for* us. This is graphically pictured for us in I John 2:1-2: "My little children, these things write I unto you, that ye sin not. And if any man sin [or is sinning], we have an advocate with the Father, Jesus Christ the righteous." Did our security rest upon our sinlessness or on our practical holiness, we would have no security whatever. But Jesus Christ, as our Advocate or Defense Attorney, at the right hand of the Father, pleads the benefits of His death and the value of His blood to cover every sin that we commit, so that the blood of Jesus Christ, God's Son, is constantly cleansing us from all sin. We have an Advocate who never slumbers nor sleeps; an Advocate who, because He is infinite in His person, can give His attention to an infinite number of children at any moment of time and can faithfully represent them as Defense Attorney before God, as need arises. We have in heaven One who appears at the right hand of the Father for us.

Jesus Christ gave to us another picture of His work, and we suggest, in the fourth place, that Christ's work *as a Shepherd* is a guarantee of our security. Not only is He faithful in heaven as an Advocate, but He is faithful here on earth as a Shepherd. We turn again to John 10 where Christ's person was challenged by the Jews. The Jews asked Christ to prove conclusively that He was the Son of God. Notice that Christ, in reply to this request, did not cite any of His great miracles, nor did He cite any of His great sermons which revealed the Father. Rather, the proof He submits that He is the Son of God is that He is able to keep His sheep. He says (vv. 27-28), "My sheep hear my voice, and I know them, and they follow me: And I give unto them eternal life; and they shall never perish, neither shall any man pluck them out of my hand." The greatest proof that Christ could offer to this Christ-rejecting nation that He was actually the Son of God was the fact that He was able to keep, to guard, to preserve His own sheep. Jesus Christ is the same yesterday, today, and forever, and the One who could preserve His own sheep when He walked among wolves can preserve His sheep today. In Hebrews 7:25 the writer says, ". . . he is able also to save them to the uttermost that come unto God by him, seeing he ever liveth to make intercession for them." He is able to save to the uttermost, not only to the bounds of time but also to the heights of privilege afforded those who are the sons of God.

In John 17 we are permitted to eavesdrop as the Son talks to the Father. In the opening portion of His prayer He talked to the Father about Himself; but in the main body of the prayer He talked to the Father about us. And the burden of His petition for us is in verses 11-16: "I am no more in the world, but these are in the world, and I come to thee. Holy Father, keep through thine own name those whom thou hast given me, that they may be one, as we are. While I was with them in the world, I kept them in thy name: those that thou gavest me I have kept, and none of them is lost, but the son of perdition; that the scripture might be fulfilled. . . . I have given them thy word; and the world hath hated them, because they are not of the world, even as I am not of the world. I pray not that thou shouldst take them out of the world, but that thou shouldst keep them from the evil [one]." When the Son communicated with the Father just before He went to the cross, and placed His petition before the Father, His last and greatest concern was for the preservation of those whom the Father had given to Him. If one of God's children is lost, if one who trusted Christ as Saviour loses his salvation, the Father denied the petition which the Son presented to the Father before He went in perfect obedience to Calvary's cross to provide the basis for our security. The provision of the Son in His death, in His resurrection, in His work as an Advocate, in His work as a faithful Shepherd guarantees our security.

The Holy Spirit is active in accomplishing our salvation, and this is a basis for the security of the child of God. The *indwelling of the Holy Spirit* is also the basis for our security, for, according to I Corinthians 6:19, these bodies have become the temple of the Holy Ghost. In Ephesians 2:22 we were made a temple in which God might dwell by the Holy Spirit. This indwelling by the Holy Spirit is never spoken of in Scripture except as a permanent indwelling; it is not temporary, not transitory. God will not abandon the temple which the Holy Spirit has constructed out of living stones, and the permanent and abiding indwelling of the Holy Spirit renders us secure.

The work of the Holy Spirit that Paul refers to in I Corinthians 12:13 as *the baptism of the Holy Spirit* makes us secure and safe. By that baptizing work we were placed in the body of Christ; we were placed as living members in the body of which Christ is the head. According to Ephesians 5:27, Christ has purchased to Himself a bride; He has sanctified and cleansed it with the washing of water by the word, "That he might present it to himself a glorious church, not having spot, or wrinkle, or any such thing; but that it should be holy and without blemish."

It must be obvious to you that if Jesus Christ purchased for Himself a bride made up of a great multitude of individual believers, and part of those believers lost their salvation, the bride presented by the Father to Christ would be imperfect and defective. Thus, it could not be said that it was without blemish. When Jesus Christ will receive a bride as a love-gift of the Father, there will be no members missing. There will be no deformity brought about by defection. There will be none who were once in the body and who have been excised from the body, so that the body is incomplete or lacking in a single part. The baptizing work of the Spirit that places us in the body of Christ is a guarantee of our security.

Finally, the work referred to in Ephesians 1:13-14 as *the sealing work of the Spirit* makes us secure. The Apostle says, ". . . ye were sealed with that holy Spirit of promise, Which is the earnest [or the down payment, the foretaste] of our inheritance until the redemption of the purchased possession, unto the praise of his glory." God has placed His identifying mark upon every child of God. This is an irremovable mark. It is an identifying brand, if you please, by which God certifies His ownership of each one who has placed faith in Jesus Christ. God the Holy Spirit is that seal which identifies us as God's possession. The plan of God the Father, the provision of God the Son, the power of God the Holy Spirit all render the child of God as secure in Christ Jesus.

This truth is quite graphically illustrated in the Old Testament. In Genesis 6, it was God's revealed purpose to send a great judgment upon the earth because of the sin and wickedness of the human race. God provided a salvation, or a way of escape, from the judgment for those who would trust Him. Noah was told (Genesis 6:14): "Make thee an ark of gopher wood. . . ." And then (6:16), Noah was commanded to make a door of the ark: ". . . the door of the ark shalt thou set in the side thereof. . . ." And then (7:7) Noah was commanded to enter the ark, and we read, "Noah went in, and his sons, and his wife, and his sons' wives with him, into the ark, because of the waters of the flood." And those who were within the ark were secured by God, for we read (7:16), ". . . they that went in, went in male and female of all flesh, as God had commanded him: and the Lord shut him in."

God provided a way of escape; it was available to all who would enter it by faith. There was no refuge outside of the ark which God provided. God himself secured those who were in the ark, and they were as secure as the ark itself.

I remember Dr. Ironside teaching the Book of Genesis in my student days. He vividly called to our attention the fact that when God caused Noah to build the ark, He did not instruct Noah to drive a peg into the side of the ark and hold on, and that if he held out to the end he would be saved. God provided a door and commanded Noah to enter the door, and then God Himself secured those who took refuge in the ark. If you have taken refuge in the Ark—Jesus Christ—you have been secured by God the Father, and God the Son, and God the Holy Spirit. You are as secure as the ark in which you rest. That is why the Apostle John said, ". . . as he is, so are we in this world" (I, 4:17). As Jesus Christ could never be brought into judgment for sin again, because His death was sufficient and complete, no more can you be brought into judgment again if you have taken up your position in the Ark, Christ Jesus. Christ said "I am the door: by me if any man enter in, he shall be saved . . ." (John 10:9). We would invite you to come into the ark and to rest in the security which God affords those who take up refuge in Him. If you do not know Jesus Christ as your personal Saviour, we invite you to receive Him and to rest in the security guaranteed by the plan of the Father, the provision of the Son, and the power of the Spirit.

13 • Predestination

Romans 8:28-39

THERE ARE FEW doctrines in the Word of God about which there has been so much heat and so little light as the doctrine of predestination. It has divided students of the Scriptures down through the ages, and theologians are wont to classify themselves on the basis of their interpretation of this one doctrine. On the one hand, there are those who emphasize the love of God and the freedom of the human will, and deprive God of sovereign authority over His creation and the right to predetermine the course of His creatures. On the other hand, there are those who so emphasize the predeterminative program of God that God is almost removed from the scene and all things work according to fixed, inexorable law and deliver us into the hands of fatalism. It is our desire to try to steer a middle course between these two extremes and present that which we believe to be the teaching of the Scriptures concerning this important doctrine.

These doctrines of the Word of God were not given to confound and to cloud the thinking of God's children, but rather they were given for our comfort and encouragement. Because we have not understood God's working in foreordination and predestination and election, we have been robbed of one of the comforting doctrines of the Word of God. There has been a tendency, on the part of men, to try to rationalize the Scriptures and to determine how they think God ought to work, instead of examining the Scriptures to see what they say as to how God did work. It is a natural tendency to humanize God; that is, to confine God to the limits of our thinking, and to preclude God from working outside the bounds of the limitations to which we are subject. But the Word of God does not confine God to the limits of men, nor does the Word of God withhold truth because it may be beyond the ability of the human mind to comprehend. As we come to predestination and these related doctrines, we are admittedly dealing with that which the natural mind is unable to comprehend. It is impossible that an infinite God could be compressed within the confines of the finite mind any more than an ocean could be compressed into a bucket. With our limited minds we are trying to understand an infinite and eternal God. It is our basic conviction, as we approach the Scriptures and these important doctrines, that God is bigger than the mind of man. May the Spirit of God deliver us from our preconception and from the limitations which we naturally would put upon God because of the limitations to which we are subject, and give us some comprehension of the working of the God who does all things for His own glory.

It is impossible to consider the doctrine of predestination without considering some related doctrines and words. To many of us such words as foreordination, predetermination, foreknowledge, election, predestination, and calling are used interchangeably, or synonymously. Doctrinally, each word is quite specific in its meaning; each one contributes something to our understanding of the working of God to glorify Himself. And until we are able to trace a logical process revealed through these words, we will always be cloudy in our thinking. While there is no chronological progression, there is a logical progression in the outworking of the eternal plan and purpose of God. We would like to suggest to you a logical order in which these important words should be considered; when so understood, they will give us a clear picture of the development of God's eternal purpose.

We want to begin with the word "foreordination," or "fore-ordained." The word might be rendered into English "to determine beforehand," or "to fix beforehand." Within this word is the thought that God possesses the ability to provide, with infinite precision, the things necessary for the ongoing of this universe which He has created. God planned all the details before the work of creation. God did not create and then sit down to decide what He would do with what had been created. As a careful Architect, God planned the use to which each part of creation would be put, the use to which each member within creation would be put. This truth is presented to us in Ephesians 1:4 where the Apostle reminds us that God has chosen us in Him (that is, in Christ) before the foundation of the world; God's purpose was determined previous to the actual act of creation. This we could call "foreordination." The universe was no accident, nor was the program in the universe left to chance after it had been created. But God predetermined a purpose and a plan, and then chose just those things that would promote the purpose and plan which He had predetermined.

We recognize that God, as an Omniscient God, knew of the possibility of evil even before He brought creation into existence. God knew that evil would oppose itself to His own holiness; yet God was not responsible for the evil which came into His creation. God was not responsible for the evil which existed, and yet God was the Architect of a plan which included evil within it. God was not caught by surprise when Lucifer rebelled against Him, nor was He taken by surprise when Adam rebelled, nor was He taken by surprise when it had to be said of all creation, "There is none righteous, no, not one" (Romans 3:10). Yet God, working a predetermined plan, worked out all of the details which were necessary to the fulfillment of that plan. In Ephesians 1:5, Paul tells us that God has worked all things "according to the good pleasure of his will." Then, in verse 11, He works all things "according to the purpose of him who worketh all things after the counsel of his own will." We discover that before any creative act of God, God predetermined what His plan was, what His program was, and the means by which that plan and program would be accomplished. God's purpose was to glorify Himself, and He designed the kind of being necessary to receive the revelation of His glory, and the kind of being necessary to ascribe glory, and majesty, and dominion and power unto God. How foolish it would be for a congregation to embark upon a building program, and to begin to construct a building, without first having designed the building. What kind of a building would we have were the building committee to announce that on a certain Saturday each member of the church would be invited to bring some building materials to the lot, where mortar and nails would be provided, and all the materials would be incorporated into the building? What a monstrosity would rise on that lot! It is no less true with God; He predetermines His purpose, His goal, His aim, and His end in creation, and then God brings into existence that program which will fulfill His purpose and aim. Paul makes this very clear in I Corinthians 2:7: "But we speak the wisdom of God in a mystery, even the hidden wisdom, which God ordained before the world unto our glory." From that verse we discover that foreordination has to do with the determining of a plan before the plan is put into operation.

The second word that contributes to our understanding of the working of God is the word "decree." It does not appear in reference to God in the Scripture, but, as used theologically, it has to do with the act by which God established the certainty of what He has planned, or predetermined. By foreordination God determines what the program will be. By God's decree God establishes the certainty of that which He has foreordained. The architect which we employed to draw up the plans for our church submitted a preliminary plan. The building committee sat down and evaluated it. We were given some general idea of the cost of erecting the kind of building initially designed, and it was the unanimous decision of the building committee to abandon that plan. The plan was good, but it did not meet our needs. The committee instructed the architect to present another plan which, when presented, met with general approval and acceptance. The architect was given instructions to proceed on the basis of that plan and prepare final drawings. The buildings we now enjoy are the result.

God conceivably had a number of options as to how He would fulfill His purpose and program, but He settled upon one plan and one purpose; He established it as His plan, His purpose, and His program by an irreversible decree. Job 22:28 establishes the principle of a decree in these words: "Thou shalt also decree a thing, and it shall be established unto thee. . . ." The decree of a king finalized a course of action. When God decreed a course of action, it finalized, solidified His plan and limited God to that specific course of action in the execution of His purpose to glorify Himself. In the prophecy of Daniel 11:36 we read, ". . . the king shall do according to his will; and he shall exalt himself, and magnify himself above every god, and shall speak marvellous things against the God of gods, and shall prosper till the indignation be accomplished: for that that is determined shall be done." Daniel is recording the fact that God has issued a decree as to what His plan is; and God's decree will certainly come to fulfillment, for Daniel says, ". . . that that is determined shall be done." In Luke 22:22 it is stated, ". . . truly the Son of man goeth, as it was determined: but woe unto that man by whom he is betrayed!" The word "determined" in that passage refers to God's decree by which God established what Jesus Christ would do during His earthly ministry, in His life, and in His death.

It is to this fact that Peter refers in the Book of Acts where, in preaching to the nation Israel, he says (2:23), "Him, being delivered by the determinate counsel and foreknowledge of God, ye have taken, and by wicked hands have crucified and slain." And again, in the same vein, we read (4:27-28) ". . . of a truth against thy holy child Jesus, whom thou hast anointed, both Herod, and Pontius Pilate, with the Gentiles, and the people of Israel, were gathered together, For to do whatsoever thy hand and thy counsel determined before to be done." God had foreordained a certain program, and then God had established the certainty and irreversibility of that program by issuing a decree as to what would take place. The Apostle, proclaiming the facts concerning the death of Christ, points out that Christ's death was no accident, that Christ was not subjected, primarily, to the will of the Jews nor the will of the Gentiles, but that the Jews and the Gentiles were doing that which God—who had foreordained the course of events—had settled and established by His decree would certainly come to pass. God in foreordination lays the plan and program; God, by His decree and His determinative counsel, establishes the certainty of that program.

That leads us logically to the third word which contributes to our understanding of the working of God—"foreknowledge." We have to draw a distinction in Scripture between God's omniscience and what God foreknows. God is a God who is all-wise, who knows with certainty the course of all events, past, present, and future. God is an omniscient God; yet foreknowledge is not synonymous with God's omniscience. Foreknowledge, as used in Scripture, refers to what God knows with certainty will come to pass because He has decreed that event. God knows all things, not only because He is an omniscient God, but because God by His decree has settled and established what will come to pass in fulfillment of His predetermined program. Foreknowledge, then, is the result of God's foreordination, or God's decree, of what would take place. God foreknows, not only what will take place, but the people who will be instruments in the fulfillment of His plan and His program. Foreknowledge has to do not only with *what* will take place but *who* will be included within the scope of God's program.

It is that thought that is in mind when the Apostle writes to the Romans and says (8:29), ". . . whom he did foreknow, he also did predestinate to be conformed to the image of his Son. . . ." It is perhaps in connection with this verse, and in connection with the word "foreknowledge," that we have run into most of the difficulty in our interpretation. A widely-held interpretation is that God has elected those who He knows will accept Christ as personal Saviour. This is an erroneous interpretation, for if God elected those who He knew beforehand would accept Him as Saviour, then God has not foreordained, God has not decreed, God has not foreknown; but rather, God has exercised His omniscience, and has limited Himself by the will of man. God is no longer a sovereign God if He elects those who He knew would accept Him as a Saviour, those who would put faith in His Son, the Lord Jesus Christ. God is then subject to the whims of the human will, and God cannot act upon, nor go beyond, the limits of the human will. Rather, what the Apostle writes in Romans 8:29 is the fact that God did know who would be included in His plan because He had foreordained and decreed that they would be included.

We find the same truth is presented in I Peter 1:2 where Peter says that we were elect according to the foreknowledge of God. May I point out to you what Peter did not say? He did not say that we are elect because of the foreknowledge of God; that is, Peter is not saying, "God looked down upon the human race, and God said, 'I see faith and I will elect those in whom I see faith.'" Rather, Peter teaches that we were "Elect according to the foreknowledge of God. . . ." The election is in keeping *with* the foreknowledge, not *because* of the foreknowledge, or *based upon* the foreknowledge. Foreknowledge says nothing of what God knew the individual would do, but foreknowledge has to do with what God knew He would do with men. God foreordained; that is, He drew the plan. God, by His decree or by His determination, settled, solidified, and finalized the plan. Consequently, God in foreknowledge knows what He will do because of His foreordination and His decree.

That brings us to the fourth important word, "election," which means "to call out." It has to do with selection. It has to do with separation unto Himself. And election has to do with the choice of the individuals who comprise those through whom the divine purpose established by foreordination will be fulfilled. God was going to work for His own glory, but God was going to work through individuals whom He separated unto Himself. And election is the sovereign work of God, according to His own purpose and will, predetermined by His foreordination, in which He selects those through whom the divine purpose will be fulfilled. We refer you again to Ephesians 1:4: we were chosen, in Christ, before the foundation of the world, that we should be holy and without blame before Him.

Election is the work of God. It is not a matter of the individual electing God, and then God electing him in response. We find this same truth presented in Romans where, concerning the national election of Israel, the divine principle in election was made very clear. The Apostle says (9:11-13), "The children [that is, Jacob and Esau] being not yet born, neither having done any good or evil, that the purpose of God according to election might stand, not of works, but of him that calleth; It was said unto her, The elder shall serve the younger. As it is written, Jacob have I loved, but Esau have I hated." This passage is very important to an understanding of the doctrine of election. You will notice that God is the One doing the electing; further, election was based upon the sovereign will of God. It was not God's response to good or evil in the one elected, for this election took place while the twins were in the womb of their mother, before either had done good or evil as the basis for His selection or rejection. Election was to fulfill the purpose of God. God's foreordained plan was the reason for God's election of Jacob. God has separated unto Himself those through whom His program would be fulfilled.

This word has suffered from much misconception, for the picture is commonly drawn of a capricious God who brings all men (who are in a neutral state) before Him, and arbitrarily says to some men, "I accept you to Myself"; and to the rest of men, "I condemn you to hell forever." Observe that when God elects, God elects out of men who were lost. Election does not separate some unto heaven and some unto hell. Election separates from among men, all of whom are under condemnation, some to fulfill God's purpose and program. Election is of grace because all men were under the curse and the wrath of God. God, to fulfill His predetermined, foreordained, decreed program, has selected those instruments He chooses to use by which that purpose and program should come to fulfillment. That any man should have been elected by God is a manifestation of the infinite grace of an infinite God.

The next word following election is "predestination," which means "to determine beforehand." This has to do with the end to which those who have been elected are set apart. This word, when used in Scripture, is always qualified by a statement of the end or the aim in view. In Ephesians 1:4-5 we read, "According as he hath chosen us in him before the foundation of the world, that we should be holy and without blame before him in love: Having predestinated us unto the adoption of children. . . ." He predestinated us—and what was the end, or the aim? The adoption of children. Notice it again in verse 11: "In whom also we have obtained an inheritance, being predestinated according to the purpose of him who worketh all things after the counsel of his own will." Predestinated—for what end? To obtain an inheritance. See it in Romans 8:29: "For whom he did foreknow, he also did predestinate [and what was the end?] to be conformed to the image of his Son. . . ." Or we see it again in I Corinthians 2:7 where we were predestinated unto glory. The Apostle says, ". . . which God ordained before the world unto our glory." From these Scriptures we would emphasize again the important fact that when predestination is used in the Scriptures it determines the end, or the goal in view, for those whom God has elected unto Himself. I find no place in Scripture where it is said that we were predestinated to faith, that we were predestinated to belief, or that we were predestinated to accept Christ. No—we were predestinated for glory. We were predestinated unto sonship or inheritance.

The word "predestination" is logically followed by the word "called," which is to be understood in its normal designation in which God summons those whom He has foreknown, those whom He has elected, those whom He has predestinated, unto Himself. The call of God to the elect of God—who have been predestinated unto glory—is the consummating act of God's foreordination. God sees to it that His purpose will be accomplished. Those whom He has chosen for Himself will be brought to Himself, that His foreknown and predetermined program might be brought to consummation. The Apostle, in Romans 8:30, said, "Moreover whom he did predestinate, them he also called: and whom he called, them he also justified: and whom he justified, them he also glorified." The call, then, is a summons to Himself, because they have been predestined unto glory by His foreordained purpose and program.

God's call is not a call to the human will, asking the human will, unaided by divine grace, to respond. God's call is also God's enablement; and God, who issues the call, imparts the power through the ministry of the Holy Spirit to respond to that call, so that the sinner who is dead, who is without life, who is under condemnation and judgment, may hear God's call; and although he has no power in himself because he is dead, and no desire to respond because God has been put out of his life, he is enabled by the Holy Spirit to respond to the gracious invitation: "Whosoever will may come." Christ made it very clear that the call was part of God's purpose and program, for in John 6:44 He said, "No man can come to me, except the Father which hath sent me draw him. . . ." And the drawing of the Father is the call of the Father to those who have been elected by God's grace, to those who have been predestinated or set apart unto glory, to those who God had foreknown would be the instruments to accomplish His foreordained purpose, which is settled and sure by the eternal and unchangeable decree of God.

Does this mean that the sinner has no responsibility? Far from it, for Christ has died for the sins of the world. Christ has made a propitiation, or a covering over, for the sins of the world. Our Lord said, "For God so loved the world, that he gave his only begotten Son, that whosoever believeth in him shall not perish, but have everlasting life" (John 3:17). The "whosoever" is unlimited. While only those whom God has called will respond to God's call, yet God's invitation is extended to all men. All men were rendered savable by the death of Christ, but only those will respond whom God calls to Himself through His efficacious grace.

If you are without Jesus Christ, there is only one thing that keeps you from Him, and that is the response of your will to the invitation which God gives when He says, "Whosoever believeth in Him should not perish, but have everlasting life." If you know Jesus Christ as your Saviour, the desire of your heart will be that of which Peter speaks in II Peter 1:10: ". . . give diligence to make your calling and election sure. . . ." The child of God who grows in grace and in the knowledge of our Lord and Saviour Jesus Christ, and who submits himself to God and his Father through Christ, has evidence within himself that he is truly a child of God.

To me the truth we have presented is one of the most comforting of all the doctrines in the Word of God. We delight to know that nothing happens by chance. We are not creatures subject to circumstances, dependent upon luck. There is no such thing as "good luck" for the child of God. An infinite, sovereign God, has *foreordained* every minute detail of our lives from before the foundation of the world. God has settled His purpose and His program by His unalterable *decree*. God *foreknows* exactly what will take place each moment of each day in our lives because it has been determined according to His purpose. God has elected us, not because of what we have done, but because it suited His infinite purpose. God, who has elected us, has set us apart by *predestination* to share His glory forever. God, in infinite grace, *called* us out of night into His love, out of death into His life, and set us apart unto Himself, not because of what we are, but because it suited God's eternal, sovereign purpose so to do. Every moment of every day we are under His care because He is working all things according to the counsel of His own will, so that we might be found unto the praise of the glory of His grace. In this confidence we rest.

14 ◆ Resurrection

I Corinthians 15:1-25

DEATH WAS NOT a part of God's original creation, but physical and spiritual death came into God's creation because of the disobedience of Adam. When God placed Adam and Eve in the Garden of Eden He put restrictions upon them which required obedience to God's revealed will. God said (Genesis 2:16-17), "Of every tree of the garden thou mayest freely eat: But of the tree of the knowledge of good and evil, thou shalt not eat of it: for in the day that thou eatest thereof thou shalt surely die."

Physical and spiritual death came into God's creation because of Adam's sin, and man immediately began to face the question, "Is there life after death?" Will there be a time when the hopes, the aspirations, the unrealized dreams, the unappropriated promises will ever be realized? And Job the Patriarch voiced that which is a universal cry of men's hearts: "If a man die, shall he live again?" (14:14).

The Old Testament gives promise of resurrection. In the very sentence in which we find Job's question we find the answer, for Job says, ". . . all the days of my appointed time will I wait, till my change come." Then, later in the book, Job says, "I know that my redeemer liveth, and that he shall stand at the latter day upon the earth: And though after my skin worms destroy this body, yet in my flesh shall I see God: Whom I shall see for myself, and mine eyes shall behold, and not another; though my reins be consumed within me" (19:25-27). To Job had been given the promise that though the flesh would see corruption, that same flesh would be brought by resurrection to see God again.

The Prophet Isaiah gives the same hope when he says (26:19), "Thy dead men shall live, together with my dead body shall they arise. Awake and sing, ye that dwell in dust: for thy dew is as the dew of herbs, and the earth shall cast out the dead." And the Prophet Daniel adds his testimony (12:2-3): ". . . many of them that sleep in the dust of the earth shall awake, some to everlasting life, and some to shame and everlasting contempt. And they that be wise shall shine as the brightness of the firmament; and they that turn many to righteousness as the stars for ever and ever."

Christ, in John 5:28-29, taught: ". . . the hour is coming, in the which all that are in the graves shall hear his voice, And shall come forth; they that have done good, unto the resurrection of life; and they that have done evil, unto the resurrection of damnation."

We find that Christ states the same truth again in John 11. At the time of the death of Lazarus, Christ came into the home of Mary and Martha in Bethany and said to Martha, "Thy brother shall rise again" (v. 23). And Martha, in good theological orthodoxy, said unto Him, "I know that he shall rise again in the resurrection at the last day" (v. 24). Living before the resurrection of Christ, Mary and Martha had an assurance from the Old Testament of the fact of resurrection. The writer to the Hebrews gives us a list of the cardinal doctrines of the Old Testament. According to Hebrews 6:2 one of the principal teachings of the Old Testament was the teaching on the resurrection of the dead. These are but a few of the many Scriptures that we could point out to you from the Old Testament concerning the confidence that God gave that, if a man die, he would live again.

From the Old Testament we learn these facts. First, there is resurrection from the dead. Second, resurrection is universal; it is for all men. Third, there are two kinds of resurrection: there is resurrection unto life and resurrection unto death; there is resurrection for the righteous and resurrection for the wicked.

We notice another fact from the Old Testament: not only would men rise to live again, but Jesus Christ, God's Messiah, God's Son, would be resurrected from the dead. In Isaiah 53 we have the prophecy of His death. In Psalm 22 we also have the prophecy of Christ's death. But these prophecies of Christ's death are accompanied by prophecies of Christ's resurrection. For instance, in Psalm 16:9-11, David says, ". . . my heart is glad, and my glory rejoiceth:

my flesh also shall rest in hope. For thou wilt not leave my soul in hell; neither wilt thou suffer thine Holy One to see corruption. Thou wilt shew me the path of life: in thy presence is fulness of joy; at thy right hand there are pleasures for evermore." Lest we think that David is speaking of himself when he says, "Thou wilt not suffer Thine Holy One to see corruption," read from Acts 2:30-31 where we have Peter's interpretation of David's prophecy in Psalm 16. After quoting this verse from Psalm 16, Peter says, "Therefore being a prophet, and knowing that God had sworn with an oath to him, that of the fruit of his loins, according to the flesh, he would raise up Christ to sit on his throne; He seeing this before spake of the resurrection of Christ, that his soul was not left in hell, neither his flesh did see corruption." Thus we have the explanation of David's prophecy of Psalm 16; it was a prophecy of the physical resurrection of Christ. Or again, in Psalm 22, David described the crucifixion of Christ; and then in verses 22-23 he says, "I will declare thy name unto my brethren: in the midst of the congregation will I praise thee. Ye that fear the Lord, praise him; all ye the seed of Jacob. . . ." Here we again have prophecy of the resurrection of Christ.

Once again, in Psalm 118, the Psalmist speaks of the resurrection of Christ (vv. 22-24): "The stone which the builders refused is become the head stone of the corner. This is the Lord's doing; it is marvellous in our eyes. This is the day which the Lord hath made; we will rejoice and be glad in it." And the Apostle Peter quotes these verses and refers it to the resurrection (I,2) of Christ and explains that "the day which the Lord hath made" is the day of resurrection, for that marvelous thing which God hath done that brings praise unto Himself is to raise Jesus Christ from the dead.

Thus far in our study we have seen that Job's question, "If a man die, shall he live again?" is answered first by teaching that men will be raised from the dead, and second, that Jesus Christ will be raised from the dead. This is by way of prophecy.

When we come over to the New Testament we find that prophecy gives way to promise, for there is promise in the New Testament of resurrection. I want to go through several passages in Matthew's Gospel where our Lord predicts and promises His own physical resurrection. Look first, if you will, at Matthew 16:21 where we read, "From that time forth began Jesus to shew unto his disciples, how that he must go unto Jerusalem, and suffer many things of the elders and chief priests and scribes, and be killed, and be raised again the third day." In Matthew 17:22-23, ". . . while they abode in Galilee, Jesus said unto them, The Son of man shall be betrayed into the hands of men: And they shall kill him, and the third day he shall be raised again." Again, in Matthew 20:18-19, Christ said, "Behold, we go up to Jerusalem; and the Son of man shall be betrayed unto the chief priests and unto the scribes, and they shall condemn him to death, And shall deliver him to the Gentiles to mock, and to scourge, and to crucify him and the third day he shall rise again." Now the same Christ who predicted His rejection, His betrayal, His crucifixion, and His burial, also predicted His resurrection. One was as much a part of Christ's promise as the other, and Christ, who knew the facts of His death, knew also the facts of His resurrection. So Christ in His earthly ministry predicted and promised His physical resurrection.

We might raise the question, "Why should Jesus Christ be raised from the dead?" I want to give you a number of references from the Word of God that explain why Jesus Christ was raised from the dead. If you turn to Acts 2:22-24, Peter, preaching on the Day of Pentecost, declares the truth of the resurrection of Christ from the dead: "Ye men of Israel, hear these words: Jesus of Nazareth, a man approved by God among you by miracles and wonders and signs, which God did by him in the midst of you, as ye yourselves also know: Him, being delivered by the determinate counsel and foreknowledge of God, ye have taken, and by wicked hands have crucified and slain: Whom God hath raised up, having loosed the pains of death: because it was not possible that he should be holden of it." The first great reason given by the Scripture for the resurrection of Christ from the dead was that the resurrection was God's great sign to the nation Israel and to the world that Jesus Christ was the Son of God, was God's heaven-sent Messiah, and the Saviour. The Apostle Peter pointed out in Acts 2:22 that Jesus was a Man approved of God, or a Man who was authenticated by God. God had put His stamp of genuineness upon Christ, and God's stamp was the miracle that Christ had risen. Throughout Christ's early life, He had worked miracles in the physical realm; He had healed the sick, the lame, the blind, the dumb, the deformed, the diseased of all kinds. Christ demonstrated that He had power over sickness and disease. Christ also raised the dead; He had power over death. He stilled the storm, He brought peace and tranquillity to the storm-tossed sea of Galilee; He had power over nature. Christ cast demons out of men, showing He had power over Satan and Satan's kingdom and the power of darkness. Christ worked these miracles to show the exceeding greatness of His power. The nation looked on Him and said, "We think He gets His power from hell; Satan gives this Man His authority. We do not believe He is the Son of God at all." The leaders of the Jews came to Christ and said, "If You are really God's Son, the Messiah, give us a confirmation of the truth; give us a sign from heaven." They remembered that the Old Testament prophet had caused the sun to stand still and had caused the heavens to withhold the rain—they were signs in heaven. Now they asked Christ to do the works of Moses and Elijah and Elisha. And Christ said, " . . . there shall be no sign given to it, but the sign of the prophet Jonas" (Matthew 12:39). For Jonah was three days and nights in the belly of the great fish and the Son of God will be three days and three nights in the earth, and He will come forth as Jonah came forth; the earth will vomit Him out as the great fish vomited Jonah out. As Jonah went in resurrection power to preach to the men in Ninevah, to bring them to a knowledge of God, so shall Jesus Christ have a message to deliver that shall bring men to God. Resurrection was to be the great authenticating sign that Jesus Christ was the Son of God.

In Romans 1:4, Paul said that the controversy as to the person of Jesus Christ was forever settled; He was "declared to be the Son of God with power, . . . by the resurrection from the dead." The resurrection of Christ is God's great answer to men's unbelief; it is a fact that cannot be denied or gainsaid. Christ arose from the dead; that is the best-attested fact of history. And God uses the resurrection as His great authenticating sign, "This is My beloved Son in whom I am well pleased." The first reason Scripture gives for the resurrection of Christ was that it was God's authentication of the person of Jesus Christ.

The second reason is given to us in Acts 2:25-31, as Peter quotes Psalm 16 and then refers it to the resurrection of Christ. He said (vv. 30-31), ". . . being a prophet, and knowing that God had sworn with an oath to him, that of the fruit of his loins, according to the flesh, he would raise up Christ to sit on his throne; He seeing this before spake of the resurrection of Christ, that his soul was not left in hell, neither his flesh did see corruption." Christ was raised from the dead to fulfill the Old Testament prophecy. It was not possible that a single line of God's Word should fail or be in error. The Old Testament had predicted the resurrection of Christ; therefore, the New Testament records the resurrection in fulfillment of the prophecy of the Word of God. It is God's authentication both of the person of Christ and the Word of God which revealed the resurrection of Christ.

The third reason for the resurrection is given us in I Corinthians 15:45 where the Apostle says, "The first man Adam was made a living soul; the last Adam was made a quickening [or life-giving] spirit." Adam was created a living thing, but he did not have the power to bestow life upon another. He could reproduce his life, but he could not create life. Therefore, when Adam's sons were born spiritually dead, Adam could not make them spiritually alive. But Jesus Christ, by the resurrection from the dead, became the One who bestowed life upon men who were both physically and spiritually dead. And so the Apostle says in I Corinthians that Christ was raised to bestow life—physical life and spiritual life—upon men.

A fourth reason is given to us in Ephesians 1:19-20: Christ was raised from the dead in order that He might impart power to men. Paul prays for these believers, that they might know "what is the exceeding greatness of his power to us-ward who believe, according to the working of his mighty power, Which he wrought in Christ, when he raised him from the dead, and set him at his own right hand in the heavenly places." Again, writing in the Epistle to the Romans (6:4), Paul says, ". . . we are buried with him by baptism into death: that like as Christ was raised up from the dead by the glory of the Father, even so we also should walk in newness of life." Christ was raised from the dead to impart His power to men who believed, in order that we might live by resurrection power. God has called upon His children to reproduce the life of Jesus Christ in their daily experience. We cannot do it of ourselves, but God has power to give us. The power of the resurrection is the power that can empower us day by day.

In Ephesians 1:22-23 we find a fifth reason: Paul says that God "hath put all things under his feet, and gave him to be the head over all things to the church, Which is his body. . . ." All believers in Christ are placed in the body of Christ; they are joined in a body of which Christ is the head. This is a figure used to teach the vital relationship which exists between Christ and the new believer. Our body is composed of many different members, yet it is one body; there is diversity in the unity. But the life that is in one part of the body is the life that is in every part of the body. There is only one kind of life in this physical body, and the life which is in the head is in the hand and the foot and the mouth. The Apostle, in I Corinthians 12, applies this to our relationship to Christ and says that we are members of His body—some of us are eyes, some of us ears, some of us hands, some of us feet—but He is the Head. He is the directive Agent. Life is in Him and life flows from Him as the Head through every member of the body. Paul, in Ephesians 1: 22-23, tells us that it was at the resurrection that Jesus Christ was made Head of the body so that believers subsequently might be united to Him. Christ was resurrected to become Head of the body.

In Ephesians 4:8, Paul gives another reason: "When he ascended up on high, he led captivity captive [or we could translate it, 'He led captive those who were held captive'], and gave gifts unto men." In verse 11 we read, "He gave some, apostles; and some, prophets; and some, evangelists; and some, pastors and teachers; For the perfecting of the saints, for the work of the ministry." What Paul teaches here is that when Christ ascended into glory He had gifts to give, just as a victorious general has spoils to give to those who were members of his army. And the gifts that God gives to His church are men—gifted men, some of whom could do the work of a prophet, the work of an apostle, the work of an evangelist, and the work of a pastor-teacher so that the saints might themselves be built up to do the work of the ministry, or to do God's work. The resurrection, then, was for the purpose of dispensing gifts to the church.

In Romans 4:25 we have the seventh reason for the resurrection: Paul tells us that Christ was delivered—that is, delivered over to death—for our offenses, and was raised again for our justification. Or, to translate it literally from the original text, "He was raised again because our justification had been accomplished." When Jesus Christ went to death for our offenses He paid to God the debt that we owed. They were *our* offenses, not His, that put Him on the cross. It was because a basis had been laid whereby God might accept us and account us as righteous that Jesus Christ was raised on the resurrection morning. Paul tells us that Christ was raised again because the basis of our justification has now been laid, and there is a sure foundation upon which we may be built; there is a basis upon which God may forgive sins.

Lastly, Christ was raised from the dead in order that He might be the first fruits of a resurrection. We read in I Corinthians 15:23: "Christ [is] the firstfruits; afterward they that are Christ's at his coming." The term "firstfruits" is used of a harvest; the first sheaf garnered out of the field at the time of the harvest promises more of the same to follow. When Christ was raised from the dead, physically, He was the firstfruits of resurrection. It was a public notice that there was a great harvest of more of the same to follow. It is the promise of our resurrection.

We can give these eight reasons from the Scriptures as to why it was not possible that death should continue to claim the body of Jesus Christ. He was raised to authenticate His person, to fulfill prophecies, to bestow life upon men, to impart power to men, to become Head of the church, to impart gifts to the church, because justification has been accomplished, and that He might be the first-fruits of a great harvest.

Not only does the New Testament give us the promise concerning the resurrection of Christ but it also gives us the promise of our physical resurrection. John's Gospel presents the words of our Lord more fully than any of the Gospels. Note several promises that Christ Himself made. First of all, in John 5:26-29: "For as the Father hath life in himself; so hath he given to the Son to have life in himself; And hath given him authority to execute judgment also, because he is the Son of man. Marvel not at this: for the hour is coming, in the which all that are in the graves shall hear his voice, And shall come forth; they that have done good, unto the resurrection of life; and they that have done evil, unto the resurrection of damnation." You will notice that Christ here teaches universality of resurrection: all that are in the graves—saved and unsaved, good and bad—shall hear His voice and shall come forth.

In John 6:39 we read, "This is the Father's will which hath sent me, that of all which he hath given me I should lose nothing, but should raise it up again at the last day. And this is the will of him that sent me, that every one which seeth the Son, and believeth on him, may have everlasting life: and I will raise him up at the last day." Now here is a remarkable truth. God the Father hath given to God the Son not only the souls of believers but the bodies in which those souls dwelt, as well. You see, God is not the least bit interested in disembodied spirits, for a disembodied spirit has no means of communication, no means of fellowship, no means of recognition. God promised the Son a gift. Redeemed men were God's gift of love to His son. God gave not only the redeemed souls but the bodies that would be redeemed by resurrection. That is what Christ means when He says, ". . . that of all which he hath given me I should lose nothing." A surgeon may have to amputate this little finger, but Christ says that of all He hath given me, I will lose nothing. So that little finger will be restored to the body in the resurrection because Christ said it will be complete. This reveals the power and authority of Christ to resurrect men.

In John 11:25-26, Christ said, "I am the resurrection, and the life: he that believeth in me, though he were dead, yet shall he live: And whosoever liveth and believeth in me shall never die." In John 14:19, Christ said, ". . . because I live, ye shall live also." These are but a few of many references to which we could direct you to let you see that Christ spoke frequently and repeatedly of the fact of our resurrection.

We want to point out to you some facts about the doctrine of the resurrection as we find it in I Corinthians 15. This, you will recognize immediately, is the great chapter on the resurrection. Paul said in verse 3: "I delivered unto you first of all that which I also received. . . ." Paul was summarizing his gospel, or his good news. Now, what is the good news which Paul preached? It has two facts: the first (v. 3): Christ died for our sins, according to the Scriptures. Since man owed God a debt, that debt must be paid before man could be accepted by God. Paul's first good news to men was that our debt has been paid, paid by Another, paid by our Substitute, paid to the full, so that the One who paid our debt could say, "It is finished." Now, what is the proof that Christ died for our sins? Verse 4 tells us: He was buried; the burial of Christ is proof of the death of Christ. The second great fact in Paul's good news is in verse 4: " . . . he rose again the third day according to the scriptures." What is the proof that Christ rose from the dead? Verse 5: ". . . he was seen of Cephas [that is, Peter]"; second, "then [He was seen] of the twelve;" the third proof was that He was seen of above five hundred brethren at once; the fourth proof (verse 7) was that He was seen of James; the fifth proof was that He was seen of all the apostles; the sixth proof was that He was seen of Paul, as one born out of due time.

I notice that when Paul wants to prove the fact of the death of Christ he gives just one proof—He was buried. But when he wants to prove the resurrection of Christ, he gives six different proofs. Why? It is not an uncommon thing for a man to die; that scarcely needs proof. But the world had never seen a resurrection before, and that needed proof. Men had seen restoration, for there were dead men who by divine power had been restored to life; but they were restored to die again. Lazarus was raised from the dead but that was not resurrection because Lazarus was raised to die again. Is that what is going to happen in the resurrection? Oh, no! In the resurrection we will receive a new, glorified, eternal body. In II Corinthians 5:1, Paul says, ". . . if our earthly house of this tabernacle were dissolved, we have a building of God, an house not made with hands, eternal in the heavens." And the new, glorified, resurrection body will be an eternal body that can never see corruption or decay. Paul recognized that, while there had been examples of restoration, there never had been an example of resurrection; therefore, he carefully documented the fact of resurrection by mentioning a number of those who had seen Him, who had touched Him, who had walked with Him, and talked with Him after He had been glorified, and they could testify to that fact.

After Paul had stated these two essential facts of his doctrine— the death of Christ and the resurrection of Christ—he began to move on to explain the doctrine of resurrection, and from verses 12 to 19 he shows to us the importance of Christ's resurrection. Notice that Paul is answering an objection. Some men might conceivably say, "I do not believe there is any such thing as resurrection because I have never seen it, nor had any evidence of it. It's something that I have to take by faith and I can't take it by faith." Paul shows the consequences if there is no such thing as resurrection from the dead. He says, first of all, that if there is no resurrection (v. 13) Christ is not risen. And if Christ is not risen (v. 14), then our preaching is in vain, or empty of content. The word "vain" in the New Testament usually means "empty," like a soap bubble. It seems to have reality but there is no reality in it at all because when you touch it, it is gone. Paul says that our preaching is just like a soap bubble if Christ isn't raised from the dead, because there is no reality to it at all. In the second place, "your faith is in vain," for you believe that Jesus is the Christ, the Son of God, and He isn't that at all if He did not rise from the dead. Third, "We are found false witnesses of God." We told a lie about God. Fourth (v. 17), ". . . ye are yet in your sins," because Christ claimed to pay a debt to God and the resurrection was God's proof that the debt had been paid—and if Jesus Christ did not rise from the dead, there was no canceled check to certify and prove that the debt had been paid. So Paul says, "If Christ has not been raised you are yet in your sins." Fifth (v. 19), "If in this life only we have hope in Christ, we are of all men most miserable." We are hopeless, we are still in sin, we have believed in vain.

After he has shown here the importance of Christ's resurrection, Paul shows the universality of resurrection. In verse 21 he says, "For since by man came death [that is, by Adam death was introduced into creation] by man [that is, Christ Jesus] came also the resurrection of the dead. For as in Adam all die, even so in Christ shall all be made alive." In Adam, how many die? *All!* Every son of Adam dies physically and spiritually. In Christ, how many will be made alive? *All!* And the two alls are equal. All men die because of Adam. All men will be brought to resurrection by Christ. This teaches the universality of resurrection. Not all will be resurrected to blessedness, but all will be resurrected.

From verse 23 through verse 34 Paul teaches us the order in resurrection. Now, we saw from the Old Testament that there would be two kinds of resurrection: resurrection unto life and resurrection unto death. Death, in that sense of the word, is separation from God. Physical death is the separation of the soul from the body. Spiritual death is the separation of the soul from God. And Daniel 12:2 and John 5:28 spoke about two kinds of resurrection: the resurrection unto life and the resurrection unto death. The resurrection unto life is often called the first resurrection. The resurrection unto death is called the second resurrection in Scripture. Do not become confused by those numbers "first" and "second." They are relative. When we understand God's program of resurrection we find that resurrection unto life, or the first resurrection, takes place in a number of stages. Notice that Paul says (I Corinthians 15:23):

". . . every man in his own order. . . ." The word translated "order" is the Greek word for "marching unit" in the Roman army, and Paul is picturing here a great triumphal procession in which a general has returned from a conflict, triumphant and victorious. He marches into the city to receive the plaudits of the people and behind him march his victorious troops. They march in ranks, in order. Now, Paul says that in the resurrection triumphal parade there will be different marching groups. First, there is the resurrection of Christ; that is referred to in verse 20: ". . . now is Christ risen from the dead, and become the firstfruits of them that slept." Christ rose from the dead. His resurrection promised a great harvest of resurrected bodies to follow Him. Christ is *a part* of the first resurrection.

If you turn to I Thessalonians 4, you find the second marching group in the triumphal procession of the resurrection. In verses 13-17 Paul says, "I would not have you to be ignorant, brethren, concerning them which are asleep, that ye sorrow not, even as others which have no hope. For if we believe that Jesus died and rose again, even so them also which sleep in Jesus will God bring with him. For this we say unto you by the word of the Lord, that we which are alive and remain unto the coming of the Lord shall not prevent them which are asleep. For the Lord himself shall descend from heaven with a shout, with the voice of the archangel, and with the trump of God: and the dead in Christ shall rise first; Then we which are alive and remain shall be caught up together with them in the clouds, to meet the Lord in the air: and so shall we ever be with the Lord." The Apostle is speaking about that which we often refer to as the rapture, or the translation, of the church. At some unannounced time the Son of God is going to appear in the clouds of heaven with a shout, the voice of the archangel, and the trump of God; He is going to summon every believer of this age to Himself. Those that have fallen asleep in Christ—that is, those who have died physically—will be resurrected. Those who are alive on the earth at that moment will be caught up with the resurrected ones who are in the process of ascending to the Lord, and these translated ones will be joined with the resurrected ones into one body and so shall we ever be with the Lord. This is the hope of the believer: at any moment we may hear that shout, that invitation, to come home when the Lord appears for His own. That coming of the

Lord in the clouds to receive His own marks the second great stage in the first resurrection. The resurrection of Christ was the first-fruits; those who are Christ's at the rapture are a part of the first resurrection.

If you turn to Revelation 20, you find a third step, or the third marching group, in the resurrection triumphal parade. In verse 4 we read, "I saw thrones, and they sat upon them, and judgment was given unto them: and I saw the souls of them that were beheaded for the witness of Jesus, and for the word of God, and which had not worshipped the beast, neither his image, neither had received his mark upon their foreheads, or in their hands; and they lived [and that word 'lived' is the Greek word which means 'resurrected'] and reigned with Christ a thousand years." In verse 6 we read, "Blessed and holy is he that hath part in the first resurrection: on such the second death hath no power, but they shall be priests of God and of Christ, and shall reign with him a thousand years." Daniel 12:2 tells us that after the tribulation period is over, when the Son of God comes to this earth to reign, He will resurrect all the Old Testament saints and bring them with Him into the glory of His millennial reign on this earth. In Hebrews 12:10 we find that Abraham looked for a city whose builder and maker is God. He was anticipating this resurrection.

Scripture also teaches that there is another part of the resurrection program. According to Revelation 20:5: ". . . the rest of the dead [that is, the unsaved dead] lived not again until the thousand years were finished." At the time that Christ comes back to this earth to reign, He has resurrected every saved person who lived from the time of Adam to the time of the return of Christ to the earth. There is not a part of a body of a single saved person left in the grave when Christ comes back to this earth to reign. But all of the wicked dead are left undisturbed and they continue in that state of death and separation from God until after Christ's reign on this earth is ended. Then Christ completes the resurrection program by calling forth the wicked dead. They are the unsaved, and they are resurrected not unto life but unto judgment. This is pictured in Revelation 20:11-14: "And I saw a great white throne, and him that sat on it, from whose face the earth and the heaven fled away; and there was found no place for them. And I saw the dead, small and great, stand before God; and the books were opened: and another book was opened, which is the book of life: and the dead were judged out of those things which were written in the books, according to their works. And the sea gave up the dead which were in it; and death and hell delivered up the dead which were in them: and they were judged every man according to their works. And death and hell were cast into the lake of fire. This is the second death." Here the Apostle John pictures the close of the resurrection program. The first resurrection, the resurrection unto life and blessing, was completed before our Lord's reign on the earth, but the resurrection of the wicked to damnation did not take place until a thousand years later when Christ raised the dead to be judged and separated from Him forever.

Now, back to I Corinthians 15. Paul has marked out the orders in the program when he says in verse 23, ". . . every man in his own order: Christ the firstfruits; afterward they that are Christ's at his coming [which includes both the resurrection of saints at the rapture and those who are resurrected at the time of the second advent]. Then cometh the end [that is, the end resurrection, or the resurrection unto damnation that takes place at the beginning of eternity]."

The next fact that Paul presents (I Corinthians 15:35-50) is an explanation of resurrection. He points out two great facts here. The first is that death is a process of bringing forth new life. Using the illustration of a seed planted in the ground, he says that before the seed can reproduce and multiply itself that seed must die. Now Paul teaches that this body may go into physical death but that death is not the end of existence: it is the means of entrance into a new glorious eternal existence because God will resurrect this body and bring it into eternal glory. Therefore death is not defeat: death is not the termination, the end; it is the means of bringing this body into eternal glory.

The second great fact he presents in this section is that while there is much identity between this body and the resurrection body, yet there is a difference. This body, he says, was corrupt; the new resurrection body will be incorruptible. This is a natural body; that is a spiritual body. This is an earthly body; that is a heavenly body. This is a body sustained by blood; that is a body sustained by the Spirit. This body is related to the first Adam, under judgment and accursed; the new glorified body will be related to the second

Adam, Christ, and it is glorious. This body was fitted for the first man; the new body will be fitted for the second man. That is what Paul means when he says (v. 42), "It is sown in corruption; it is raised in incorruption: It is sown in dishonour; it is raised in glory: it is sown in weakness; it is raised in power: It is sown a natural body; it is raised a spiritual body." And the Apostle then promises us (v. 49) that "as we have borne the image of the earthy, we shall also bear the image of the heavenly."

The Apostle teaches us, in this passage, that even though there is a transformation from corruption into incorruption, the individual does not lose his identity. We will be recognizable and we will know one another. We will know the saints of the Old Testament and of the New Testament who have gone before. There will be communication between the saints.

Then the Apostle goes on, from verse 51 to 53, to give us an important exception to resurrection. From the time of Adam to the time that the Lord appears in the heavens with a shout, and the voice of the archangel and the trump of God, death has been the expectation of every individual who lived. But Paul says that there is to be an exception to this death-resurrection process; for Paul teaches that there will be one generation of believers who will go to heaven without the experience of physical death and resurrection. They will receive a new glorified body without the experience of physical death. Paul says (vv. 51-53), "I shew you a mystery [a brand-new truth hitherto unrevealed]; We shall not all sleep [that is, not all believers will die physically], but we shall all be changed, In a moment, in the twinkling of an eye, at the last trump; for the trumpet shall sound, and the dead shall be raised incorruptible, and we shall be changed. For this corruptible must put on incorruption, and this mortal must put on immortality." He says that there is coming a moment when the Lord Jesus Christ will appear in the clouds of heaven, and He will summon all believers unto Himself, and in the twinkling of an eye we will receive a new glorified body without this body having been brought into physical death, corruption, dissolution, and subsequent resurrection. So, Paul says, we have this anticipation that the Lord may come before physical death can lay hold upon us.

Paul closes this great chapter by showing us God's victory through resurrection. He says in verse 54, "So when this corruptible shall have put on incorruption, and this mortal shall have put on immortality, then shall be brought to pass the saying that is written, Death is swallowed up in victory." Then he asks two questions: "O death, where is thy sting? O grave, where is thy victory?" (v. 55). Then he answers them, "The sting of death is sin [it is sin that makes death painful]; and the strength of sin is the law. But thanks be to God, which giveth us the victory through our Lord Jesus Christ" (vv. 56-57). Death holds dread for the man who bears the guilt and the burden of his own sin, for he knows that it is appointed unto men once to die and after this the judgment. And the man who does not have the knowledge of sins forgiven knows that the next step in God's program is for him to stand before a righteous, holy God to be judged for his sins, and God's just and righteous judgment is banishment from His presence forever.

Since Jesus Christ is raised from the dead, we who have received Him as Saviour have the assurance that sins have been forgiven and that the next step in the program is resurrection into His glory—not resurrection to eternal damnation and judgment. So there is victory through the resurrection of Christ—victory over sin, victory over defeat, victory over despair, victory over fear—because Christ hath been raised and He said, "If I live, ye shall live also." This is the message of certainty and hope that we have, for the Word of God predicted Christ's resurrection, promised us our resurrection, and it explains to us God's program of resurrection. We live, not in anticipation of physical death, but in the light of God's revelation that we can live anticipating the coming of the One who will translate us into His glory. But should death be our experience, we rest in hope, for death has been robbed of its venom because Christ has been raised from the dead.